Thrive

A Leader's Guide to Organisational Culture

Dr Kevin Croker

Grosvenor House
Publishing Limited

The right of Kevin Croker to be identified as the author of this
work has been asserted in accordance with Section 78
of the Copyright, Designs and Patents Act 1988

The book cover is copyright to Kevin Croker

This book is published by
Grosvenor House Publishing Ltd
Link House
140 The Broadway, Tolworth, Surrey, KT6 7HT.
www.grosvenorhousepublishing.co.uk

A CIP record for this book
is available from the British Library

Paperback ISBN 978-1-83615-365-8
eBook ISBN 978-1-83615-366-5

Dedication

To my wife, Dawn—who encouraged me to write this book and has supported me every step of the way.

"Be still, and know that I am God." — Psalm 46:10

Acknowledgements

I would like to express my sincere gratitude to the many individuals who have influenced my understanding of organisational culture throughout my career, both as a leader and as a researcher exploring its impact on performance. Every experience, conversation, challenge, and success has contributed to shaping my perspective. We learn not only from inspiring leaders and thriving organisations but also from those who fall short. Leadership, after all, is a journey of continuous learning, and some of the most profound lessons come from moments of failure as much as from success. To those who have challenged my thinking, reinforced the importance of culture, and demonstrated, either directly or indirectly, what it truly means for an organisation to *thrive*, I extend my deepest appreciation. This book is a reflection of those experiences and insights, and I hope it serves as a valuable guide for others on their own leadership journey.

Contents

Preface

Organisational culture is something we all experience, regardless of title or tenure. Anyone who has ever worked in an organisation has felt its culture, whether or not they had a role in shaping it. Early in my career, I found myself in this exact position. Like most people starting out, I worked within the parameters of someone else's chosen culture. I quickly saw how culture, whether strong or weak, could either inspire excellence or stifle engagement, depending on how well values were aligned with real behaviours and practices.

These early observations sparked my deep interest in cultural leadership. Watching both thriving and failing cultures in action helped shape the kind of leader I aspired to be and the kind of culture I wanted to build. One truth became clear: a culture where values exist only as words, without being reflected in everyday behaviours, inevitably disengages people, erodes motivation, and weakens performance. In contrast, when culture is well-constructed, nurtured, and truly lived by leaders and employees alike, it creates a lasting, positive impact on performance, morale, and growth.

When I stepped into my first leadership role, I made a firm commitment. I would build a culture that inspired people to be part of something greater. A culture rooted in values that drove engagement, collaboration, and excellence. I knew that choosing the right values was only the first step, true success would come from embedding those values into daily behaviours at every level of the organisation. With this approach, I saw first-hand the immense power of cultural alignment. Our teams became more motivated, our organisation achieved higher levels of productivity, innovation, and customer satisfaction, and profitability soared. People didn't just work for us; they believed in what we were building together.

This experience deepened my belief in the power of culture and led me to explore its impact academically. My research focused on how culture permeates an organisation and how its alignment – or misalignment – affects performance. This led me to develop a practical methodology for measuring cultural alignment and answering a critical question: *Is the culture you have the culture you want?* My findings reinforced one key idea: leaders always get the culture they deserve. To shape a truly high-performing organisation, culture must be intentionally crafted, continuously measured, and actively reinforced.

This is why I wrote *Thrive*. My goal is to provide leaders with a practical, actionable guide to shaping, embedding, and measuring culture in a way that delivers lasting success. In these pages, I share insights, strategies, and tools to help leaders not just define their ideal culture, but ensure it is lived at every level of the organisation. Because when culture truly supports and empowers people, organisations don't just improve – they excel, sustain, and flourish.

Why the Tree? The Symbolism of *Thrive's* Cover

The cover of *Thrive* features a tree for a reason. It represents the very essence of what this book is about, creating organisations that grow, flourish, and endure. The tree is a powerful analogy for sustainable success, with its branches representing the organisation's strategic objectives. These objectives reach upward, seeking growth, innovation, and achievement. Yet the tree cannot thrive without the soil beneath it. The soil symbolises organisational culture, the foundation that nourishes and sustains the strategy. A well cultivated culture, much like rich, healthy soil, ensures that the tree can grow tall and resilient, weathering challenges and bearing fruit.

Without a strong, supportive culture, even the most ambitious strategies may falter. The tree will lack the stability and nourishment it needs to grow. On the other hand, with a vibrant and aligned culture, an organisation's strategic goals are not only achieved but sustained over time. The green colour of the cover reflects the broader theme of sustainability, not only in how organisations can maintain success but also in the relevance of environmental responsibility. In a world where sustainability is increasingly critical, it is fitting that the tree stands as a reminder of the importance of growth that is rooted in responsibility. Through this analogy, *Thrive* offers practical steps to help leaders cultivate their cultural 'soil' to support the strategic 'tree', ensuring their organisations not only succeed but truly thrive.

I hope you find this book both insightful and practical, offering the tools and inspiration needed to cultivate a thriving organisational culture that drives success and sustainability for years to come.

Introduction

Why Culture is Your Competitive Edge

Why Culture Matters Now More Than Ever

Imagine this: an organisation operates for years under a toxic culture of distrust, miscommunication, and denial. The result? Over 700 innocent people are wrongfully accused of fraud, some imprisoned, others losing their livelihoods, some even their lives. This is not a fictional tale. This is the story of the UK's Post Office scandal – a glaring example of what happens when organisational culture is neglected and leadership fails to step in.

In recent years, the Post Office faced national outrage due to a series of wrongful prosecutions against sub-postmasters, who were accused of theft and fraud based on a flawed IT system. However, this wasn't just a technological failure; it was a cultural one. The leadership ignored warnings, failed to listen to its employees, and created an environment where transparency and accountability were sidelined in favour of covering up mistakes. The CEO was heavily criticised for not fostering an environment of open communication and cultural responsibility, ultimately leading to the collapse of trust within the organisation and public confidence.

But this isn't an isolated case. Consider Uber, where a lack of accountability and a 'win-at-all-costs' mentality led to a toxic culture of sexual harassment, lawsuits, and eventual leadership shake-ups. Or Wells Fargo, where aggressive sales goals and a culture of fear drove employees to open millions of fraudulent accounts, leading to one of the biggest banking scandals in modern history. Both cases are reminders that without the right culture, even successful organisations can crumble from the inside out.

The lesson is clear. Culture is not a side issue; it's the foundation of every organisation's success or failure. Neglect it at your peril.

The senior leader of an organisation must see themselves as the chief cultural architect, the one responsible for setting, modelling, and reinforcing the values and behaviours that shape the organisation. Culture is not something that can be delegated or outsourced. It is built from the top and permeates through every level of the company. While the leader can, and should, solicit help from HR, consultants, or other departments to support the development of a thriving culture, they cannot abdicate their responsibility for it.

A healthy, sustainable culture begins with the values which the senior leader actively chooses and embodies. These values are the foundation that guides how decisions are made, how employees are treated, and how the organisation interacts with its customers and stakeholders. The leader must be deliberate in embedding their chosen values into everyday behaviours and practices, ensuring they align with the company's vision and goals.

Leaders like Satya Nadella at Microsoft have successfully reshaped their organisation's culture by being intentional about values like empathy, growth mindset, and innovation. By actively driving these values and holding themselves accountable, senior leaders can inspire others to follow suit. This top-down approach is crucial for creating a culture that encourages engagement, innovation, and resilience, one where employees are not just aligned with the company's goals but are empowered to achieve them sustainably.

In essence, the senior leader sets the tone and must consistently be the champion for the culture they want to cultivate. When leadership embraces this role, culture becomes a strategic asset that supports both short-term performance and long-term success.

The Consequences of Neglecting Culture

When leadership ignores cultural warning signs, the consequences can be devastating. The Post Office scandal, driven by a culture of silence and fear, led to a national outcry and irreversible harm. At Uber, it wasn't until employee Susan Fowler's viral blog post exposed systemic harassment that the toxic culture was addressed. By then, the damage to the company's reputation and employee morale was done. Similarly, Wells Fargo's culture of high-pressure sales not only cost the company millions in fines but also shattered trust with customers.

The consequences of neglecting culture are widespread. Employees become disengaged, productivity drops, innovation stalls, and ultimately financial performance suffers. In fact, research shows that companies with strong cultures see four times higher revenue growth than those without. Organisations with positive cultures also report greater employee retention, increased customer loyalty, and a significant boost in brand reputation.

What Organisational Culture Really Is

So, what exactly is culture? Simply put, it's 'the way we do things around here': a set of shared values, beliefs, and behaviours that shape how work gets done and determines a right and wrong way to go about it. It is how far the leaders' chosen values and resulting behaviours permeate through every level of their organisation. Culture determines how employees interact, how decisions are made, and how adaptable the organisation is in times of change. It's not just about policies or perks; it's about the collective mindset that drives every behaviour and action.

In the case of the Post Office, a culture of fear, lack of communication, and an unwillingness to address systemic issues led to one of the largest miscarriages of justice in UK history. At Uber, the unchecked toxic culture fostered harassment, leading to significant legal and financial repercussions.

But culture isn't something that just happens spontaneously. Great leaders understand that it requires intentional effort to create and sustain. Culture can be designed, shaped, and improved, and that's exactly what this book is here to help you do.

The Purpose of This Book

I've seen first-hand how powerful culture can be, both for good and for bad. My experience working with organisations facing cultural challenges has shown me that shaping a healthy, positive culture isn't just a responsibility for HR or senior management. It's something that must be led by the senior leader and which everyone in the organisation can contribute to.

That's why I wrote this book. I want to help to demystify organisational culture and give leaders, managers, and employees practical, actionable insights and tools to shape the culture they want. This is not a book full of theory. It's about making real changes that improve how your organisation operates day-to-day. Whether you're a CEO or a frontline manager, or simply have an interest in organisation culture, the concepts and insights here will help you to understand how to build a thriving culture.

What we will discuss

In the chapters ahead, we'll explore how to:

- Assess your current organisational culture and identify gaps.
- Understand the critical role that leadership plays in culture-building, as well as the role that each individual can play.

- Embed your company's values into everyday behaviours and decision-making.
- Build trust, improve communication, and foster adaptability.
- Avoid the cultural pitfalls that have caused organisations like the Post Office, Uber, and Wells Fargo to collapse into scandal and chaos.

We'll also provide practical tools you can use right away, such as:

- Leadership self-assessments to evaluate your role in shaping culture.
- Reflection exercises for teams to align values with actions.
- Practical strategies to communicate your vision and foster cultural buy-in.

Through real life examples, tools, and reflection exercises, you'll gain the insights you need to start shaping a culture that works for you and your organisation. One that attracts the best talent, retains engaged employees, and leads to sustained success.

A Call to Action

Culture is more than just words on a wall, or website, or vague ideals tucked into your mission statement. It's the very fabric that determines how your company behaves and performs, especially when under pressure.

Are you ready to stop neglecting your culture and start shaping it for success? In this book, we'll walk step by step through how to create a culture that works for your organisation and your people, helping you avoid the traps of a toxic culture like the one that brought the Post Office to its knees.

Culture is your competitive edge. Are you ready to create the one that will make your organisation thrive?

Chapter 1

Mind the Gap

Introduction: The Leadership Blind Spot

It's all too common for senior leaders to believe their organisation's culture is strong and aligned with its values. They see a thriving, innovative, and collaborative environment, or at least, that's what they expect. However, when you move down the hierarchy, the lived experience of employees can tell a very different story.

This disconnect between the intended culture and the experienced culture is what we call the 'culture gap'. It's a leadership blind spot that can undermine strategy, hinder performance, and lead to disengagement at all levels of the organisation. For many leaders, the gap is a slow, creeping problem that they only become aware of once it's too late.

The role of the senior leader is not only to set the strategic direction for the organisation but to ensure the organisation's culture is supportive of their strategy and close any cultural gaps by continuously assessing and realigning the actual culture with the desired one.

The Gap Between Vision and Reality

Culture is not just what's written in policy documents or spoken in meetings. It's the unwritten, everyday behaviours that employees experience. Leaders may believe they've created a culture of trust, yet their employees may feel silenced or fearful of raising concerns. This disconnect is what drives organisational dysfunction and disengagement.

A Common Misalignment of Culture

A telling example comes from Uber in its early years. Under the leadership of founder Travis Kalanick, the company's stated values included innovation, customer obsession, and meritocracy. Yet the reality was a toxic workplace where employees felt pressured to cut ethical corners to meet performance targets. The gap between the values espoused by Uber's leadership and the culture lived out by its employees was vast, eventually leading to public scandals and Kalanick's resignation.

Wells Fargo

Similarly, Wells Fargo's leadership believed they were fostering a customer-centric culture. However, intense pressure to meet aggressive sales quotas led employees to open fraudulent accounts to meet targets. The leadership's vision of putting customers first was completely disconnected from the behaviour driven by the organisational incentives in place, leading to one of the largest banking scandals in recent history.

In both cases, leaders were blind to the gap between their intentions and the actual culture. The consequences were severe, including damaged reputations, legal penalties, and a breakdown of trust.

How the Culture Gap Affects Performance

Organisations that fail to bridge the culture gap are often plagued by poor performance, low morale, and high employee turnover. When employees see a disconnect between what leaders say and what they do, it breeds cynicism and disengagement.

Employee Engagement

Studies by Gallup reveal that only a small fraction of employees feel truly engaged at work, and a major factor is the misalignment between company values and leadership behaviour. If the CEO talks about innovation but employees are penalised for taking risks, the result is a disengaged workforce, less creativity, and ultimately lower productivity.

Performance and Trust

The 2017 Edelman Trust Barometer showed that trust in business is eroded when there's a disconnect between what leaders say and what employees experience. Trust is a key driver of performance, collaboration, and long-term success. Without trust, employees are less likely to invest themselves fully in the organisation's mission, and high performing teams become rare.

The Hidden Costs of a Culture Gap

The culture gap often leads to higher turnover, as disengaged employees leave for organisations where they feel more aligned. The cost of replacing employees, not to mention the loss of institutional knowledge, can be significant. Furthermore, companies with a large culture gap are more prone to unethical behaviour, as the lack of clarity and alignment between values and actions creates grey areas.

The CEO's Responsibility: Closing the Gap

Recognising and closing the culture gap is a senior leader's responsibility, and it cannot be delegated to HR or middle management. The CEO must take full ownership of both the strategy and the culture of the organisation. Here's how to do it:

Awareness: Stepping Outside the Leadership Bubble

Leaders often have a skewed perception of their organisation's culture because they're not exposed to the day-to-day experiences of employees. To gain an accurate understanding, they must create opportunities for honest feedback and open communication. This might involve:

- Anonymous employee surveys that ask tough questions about how employees view the culture.
- Focus groups that allow employees from different levels to candidly discuss their experiences.

- Cultural audits conducted by external consultants who can provide objective insights.

By actively seeking out this feedback, leaders can pinpoint the areas where the culture is misaligned with their intention.

Action: Bridging the Gap with Intentional Leadership

Once leaders become aware of the gap, the next step is taking action. This doesn't mean an overnight overhaul of the organisation, but rather targeted, incremental changes that realign the culture with the desired values.

For example, if the culture gap reveals that employees feel pressured to prioritise profits over ethics, the leader might need to rethink performance metrics and incentives. Similarly, if employees report a lack of psychological safety, leadership must focus on building a culture where open dialogue and feedback are encouraged and valued.

Consistency: Living the Values Daily

Leaders must model the behaviours emanating from the values they want to see. This means leading by example and consistently reinforcing the desired behaviours. If integrity is a core value, the leader must be transparent about both successes and failures and ensure that the same level of accountability applies to everyone.

The most effective leaders close the culture gap by making values-based decisions at every level, from the boardroom to individual teams. This consistency builds trust and creates an environment where employees feel secure in the culture being developed.

Tools for Identifying and Bridging the Gap

To effectively close the culture gap, leaders need actionable tools that provide continuous feedback and accountability. Some methods to achieve this include:

- Employee Surveys and Feedback Mechanisms: These are essential for gauging how employees truly feel about the culture. The questions should go beyond satisfaction and delve into trust, alignment with values, and day-to-day experiences.
- Cultural Audits: Bringing in external experts to conduct cultural audits can provide an unbiased assessment of the gap between leadership's vision and the actual culture.
- 360-Degree Feedback for Leaders: This allows leaders to understand how their actions are perceived by others in the organisation, offering insights into whether they are effectively modelling the desired culture.
- Cultural Performance Metrics: Linking cultural outcomes to measurable business performance ensures that culture isn't seen as an abstract concept but as a real driver of success.

The Cost of Not Minding the Gap

Ignoring the culture gap comes with serious consequences, both immediate and long-term. These include:

1. Higher Turnover: Disengaged employees are more likely to leave, resulting in higher recruitment and onboarding costs.
2. Decreased Performance: Without a cohesive, aligned culture, employees are less productive and less collaborative, which impacts overall performance.
3. Reputational Damage: As seen in the Post Office and Wells Fargo examples, organisations with significant culture gaps often face public scandals, damaging both their reputation and their bottom line.

The Post Office Scandal

The recent scandal surrounding the UK Post Office is a prime example of how a culture gap can have devastating consequences. Senior leadership failed to listen to the concerns of sub-postmasters, many of whom were wrongfully prosecuted for fraud due to faulty IT systems. This scandal arose from a toxic culture where fear and a lack of transparency prevented crucial feedback from reaching the top. The Post Office leadership's failure to bridge the culture gap led to years of suffering for innocent workers and one of the most significant miscarriages of justice in recent corporate history.

Bridging the Gap: A Leadership Imperative

Closing the culture gap requires more than just awareness; it demands action and commitment from senior leaders. Here are some steps to begin bridging the gap:

- Create Transparency: Build open communication channels where employees feel safe to share their concerns without fear of retaliation.
- Align Values with Behaviours: Clearly define the behaviours that reflect the chosen values, and make sure these behaviours are visible and rewarded.
- Embed Values into Every Process: Ensure that hiring, promotions, and performance management are all aligned with the organisation's values. This means hiring for cultural fit as much as technical skill, and rewarding behaviours that support the desired culture.

Cultural Audits: A Key Tool for Diagnosing the Gap

One of the most effective ways to identify a cultural gap is through a cultural audit. This is a systematic assessment that evaluates how well the values and behaviours that define your culture align with the everyday practices of the organisation. Cultural audits involve collecting data from across the company, often through surveys, interviews, and focus groups. These tools offer valuable insights into how employees perceive leadership, values, and the overall work environment.

In a successful cultural audit, it's important to involve employees at all levels. Too often, audits focus solely on executive leadership's perspective, but this can miss the lived experiences of mid-level managers and frontline employees, who are often most affected by cultural misalignments.

Microsoft's Cultural Turnaround

When Satya Nadella took over as CEO of Microsoft in 2014, one of his key priorities was transforming the company's culture. Microsoft had developed a reputation for being competitive internally, fostering a 'cutthroat' atmosphere that stifled collaboration. Nadella recognised the cultural gap between the company's mission of driving innovation and its internal behaviour, which was hindering employee creativity and engagement.

To address this, Nadella initiated a cultural transformation by introducing a growth mindset, focusing on learning and collaboration rather than competition. He used feedback from a company-wide cultural audit to identify specific areas where the organisation's culture needed change, such as breaking down silos between departments. Nadella's efforts to close this gap led to a significant shift in employee morale and helped position Microsoft as a leader in innovation once again.

Consequences of Ignoring the Cultural Gap

Failing to address cultural gaps has both immediate and long-term repercussions. As mentioned earlier, a significant cultural gap can cause disengagement and turnover. However, the consequences can go beyond these internal challenges. A misaligned culture can damage the organisation's external reputation, alienate customers, and even lead to legal or ethical breaches.

Boeing and the 737 MAX Crisis

The Boeing 737 MAX crisis is an example of how a deep cultural misalignment can have devastating consequences. Boeing's leadership had long championed safety as one of its core values, but the rush to compete with Airbus for market share led to compromises in this area. Internal emails and reports revealed that employees felt pressured to meet aggressive deadlines, even if it meant cutting corners on safety testing.

This gap between Boeing's stated values of safety and the reality on the ground led to two catastrophic crashes involving the 737 MAX aircraft, resulting in the deaths of 346 people. Boeing's failure to live its cultural value of safety not only caused tragic loss of life but also severely damaged its reputation and financial standing.

Closing the Gap: Tools and Strategies

Closing a cultural gap requires deliberate actions that start from the top but permeate every level of the organisation. It's not enough for senior leaders to set the values; they must also ensure that middle managers and employees have the tools and support necessary to live those values in their daily work. Here are some actionable strategies:

Align Performance Metrics with Values

Often, organisations inadvertently create cultural gaps by setting performance metrics that are misaligned with their stated values. For example, if a company says it values collaboration but rewards individual achievement and competition, the culture will gravitate towards competitive behaviours. To close this gap, leaders need to ensure that key performance indicators (KPIs) are aligned with cultural values.

A company that successfully implemented this approach is Zappos, where customer service is a key cultural value. Instead of measuring call centre employees on how quickly they resolve customer inquiries, Zappos measures them on the quality of their interactions with customers. This shift has helped the company maintain a culture focused on delivering exceptional customer service, aligned with its core value of treating customers with empathy.

Role-Modelling at Every Level

While senior leaders play a pivotal role in setting the tone, role-modelling behaviour needs to happen at every level of the organisation. Middle managers are often the 'translators' of culture, as they interact directly with both senior leadership and frontline employees. Ensuring that middle managers are fully aligned with the company's values and equipped to role model desired behaviours is critical.

Procter & Gamble (P&G) has been recognised for its efforts in ensuring cultural consistency across its global operations. P&G embeds its values into leadership development programmes, training managers not only in technical skills but also in how to embody the company's core values of integrity and innovation. This focus on role modelling across the organisation helps P&G maintain a cohesive culture despite its large and diverse workforce.

Creating Safe Spaces for Feedback

One of the biggest barriers to closing cultural gaps is fear. Employees are often reluctant to provide honest feedback about cultural issues, particularly if they believe it will negatively affect their job security. Creating 'safe spaces' where employees can voice concerns about misalignment is crucial. This might involve anonymous surveys, town hall meetings, or dedicated teams tasked with gathering cultural feedback.

Google has long been a champion of creating such environments through its 'Googlegeist' survey, which allows employees to share feedback about the company's culture, leadership, and internal practices. This feedback is used to make informed decisions about organisational changes and to identify any emerging cultural gaps before they grow wider.

Closing the Culture Gap Through Active Listening

One of the most effective ways for leaders to identify and address culture gaps is through active listening. Often, the gaps between intended culture and the actual day-to-day experience of employees are not immediately visible to those in leadership positions. Employees, especially those at lower levels, can feel distant from the leadership team and may hesitate to voice their concerns or provide feedback. To bridge this divide, senior leaders must create channels where employee voices are heard, valued, and acted upon.

This could take the form of regular feedback sessions, anonymous surveys, or open-door policies, but the key is ensuring that communication flows both ways.

It's important for employees to feel psychologically safe to express their thoughts, and even more crucial for leaders to act on the feedback received. A lack of follow-up on feedback can deepen the gap, as employees may lose trust and see the initiative as mere lip service.

In organisations where employees feel they are listened to and where their input can lead to tangible change, culture permeates more naturally. The process of addressing culture gaps should not be seen as a one-off event but as an ongoing dialogue.

The Role of Internal Audits in Identifying Culture Gaps

A highly effective tool for narrowing culture gaps is the use of internal audits focused on organisational culture. These are distinct from traditional financial or compliance audits, as they specifically assess whether the behaviours, attitudes, and practices across the organisation align with its stated values. Internal audits can help uncover discrepancies in different departments, regions, or leadership levels, and highlight where the culture isn't being lived out as intended.

For example, a company that promotes teamwork as a core value may find, through an internal culture audit, that some teams are highly collaborative while others function in silos. The audit might reveal that managers in certain departments do not incentivise cross-team collaboration, leading to disconnects. Addressing this requires leadership to not only recognise the gap but also to implement targeted interventions such as revised management training or adjusted performance metrics that prioritise teamwork.

Leadership and the Power of Transparency

Another essential element in addressing culture gaps is transparency from leadership. Employees are more likely to engage with cultural initiatives when they see leaders being open about both the successes and challenges the organisation faces. Leaders who are honest about where the organisation currently stands culturally, and where it aspires to go, are far more likely to galvanise support from their teams.

Transparency also extends to admitting when cultural initiatives are not working as intended. It can be tempting for leaders to push forward with an initiative even when it's clear that it's not yielding the desired results. However, admitting when things need adjustment, and being willing to pivot, is a powerful way to show that the organisation is genuinely committed to closing the gap between its cultural goals and the reality on the ground. The gap between an organisation's intended culture and the reality that employees experience daily can be vast, and this disconnect is often where many organisations falter. This cultural gap doesn't emerge overnight but is usually the result of incremental slippage over time, with competing priorities and misaligned actions at various levels. Leaders must be vigilant in recognising when their envisioned culture no longer aligns with what is being lived out across the organisation.

The risk of ignoring this gap is immense. When employees feel a disconnect between the organisation's stated values and what they experience, it leads to disengagement. According to Gallup's research on workplace engagement, a clear organisational culture can increase employee engagement by up to 30%, leading to better performance and retention. When employees see a gap between what leadership says and what leadership does, trust erodes. This erosion of trust can have cascading effects, leading to high employee turnover, lower morale, and a weakened brand reputation.

In addressing this gap, it's important to recognise that the small things matter. Culture isn't just shaped in boardrooms and strategy meetings; it's reinforced in everyday behaviours and actions. Leaders need to continuously model the behaviours they wish to see across the organisation. This requires walking the floor, actively listening to employee concerns, and having candid conversations about where cultural gaps may exist. It's through these micro-interactions that the foundation of a healthy culture is built and maintained.

The Role of Feedback Loops in Closing the Gap

One of the key strategies for closing the cultural gap is the development of robust feedback loops. Feedback must not only be encouraged but be actively sought out. Leaders must show that they are genuinely invested in hearing from their employees and, most importantly, act on the feedback. The act of soliciting input without follow-through is more damaging than not asking for feedback in the first place. When employees feel that their input is acknowledged and acted upon, they become more invested in maintaining the culture.

Establishing two-way communication channels ensures that leaders are not operating in a bubble. Surveys, town hall meetings, and employee forums are some ways to gather this feedback. But beyond formal methods, it's often the informal touchpoints, the daily check-ins, conversations over coffee, and open-door policies that provide the most honest and insightful feedback on whether the intended culture is truly resonating at all levels of the organisation.

External Forces That Widen the Cultural Gap

Cultural gaps can also be exacerbated by external forces such as economic downturns, technological advancements, and rapid changes in market conditions. When an organisation faces external pressure, there is often a temptation to cut corners or stray from its values in the pursuit of short-term gains. For instance, during a financial crisis, an organisation that values 'people first' may suddenly find itself laying off employees en masse or cutting critical employee benefits. These actions, although perhaps necessary, can send mixed messages to employees about what the organisation truly values.

In times of external pressure, it's critical for leadership to reaffirm their commitment to their cultural values, even if the circumstances require difficult decisions. A strong culture can weather external storms if employees believe that the leadership team is making decisions with the long-term health of the organisation in mind, and not just chasing short-term wins.

A Focus on Accountability

Accountability is one of the key factors in closing the gap between the culture that leaders envision and the one which employees experience. Leaders must hold themselves, and their teams, accountable for upholding the organisation's values and ensuing behaviours. It's essential that cultural values are not just printed on posters in the office but are woven into performance evaluations, promotions, and day-to-day operations. An organisation that says it values innovation, for example, must ensure that its reward systems and leadership behaviours reflect that commitment, whether that means providing time and resources for creative thinking or celebrating risk-taking even when it doesn't always yield the desired results.

In holding people accountable, it is equally important to celebrate those who embody the organisation's values. Recognition programmes that highlight employees who live out the desired culture are effective in reinforcing behaviours and showing others what it looks like to 'close the gap' between stated and lived values.

Mind the Gap and Move Forward

Closing the cultural gap is not a one-time event but an ongoing process. As organisations grow, enter new markets, or experience leadership changes, cultural gaps can re-emerge. Leaders must remain vigilant, continually assess their organisation's culture, and adapt strategies to ensure that values and behaviours remain aligned.

Organisations that successfully bridge cultural gaps are those that treat culture as a strategic asset, not an afterthought. By choosing values that drive desired behaviours, holding themselves accountable, and regularly gathering feedback from all levels of the organisation, leaders can create a culture where employees are engaged, aligned, and positioned for long-term success.

Adapting Culture for Different Generations

Another challenge for leaders is managing the culture gap that can arise between different generations within the workforce. Today, many organisations consist of a mix of Baby Boomers, Gen X, Millennials, and Gen Z – each bringing its own values, work styles, and expectations. Leaders must recognise that a one-size-fits-all approach to culture may not be effective in such a diverse environment.

For instance, Baby Boomers may value stability, loyalty, and clear hierarchies, while Millennials and Gen Z often prioritise flexibility, innovation, and a sense of purpose in their work. The challenge for leaders is to craft a culture that resonates across these different demographics without diluting the core values of the organisation.

To close the generational culture gap, leaders should create opportunities for cross-generational mentoring, where younger and older employees can learn from each other's perspectives. Additionally, providing tailored communication and training that considers the diverse needs of each group can ensure that all employees feel valued and engaged within the culture.

Conclusion: Mind the Gap

The culture gap is a common but dangerous blind spot for many leaders. Closing it requires vigilance, self-awareness, and action. The senior leader must take responsibility for both the vision and the day-to-day reality of the organisational culture. By minding the gap, leaders can create an environment where values are lived, performance thrives, and strategic goals are achieved in a sustainable way.

Reflection: Questions for Leaders

As you strive to close the culture gap, reflect on the following questions:

- How do I know if there's a gap between the culture I envision and the culture my employees experience?
- What feedback mechanisms do I have in place to get an honest view of the organisation's culture?
- How am I actively closing this gap through my own actions and leadership?
- What can I do to ensure that our values are being lived out at every level of the organisation?

Chapter 2

Values as the Foundation of Organisational Culture

Organisational culture is often described as 'the way things are done around here'. But it runs much deeper. It's the heartbeat of an organisation, influencing everything from daily decision-making to long-term success. At the core of this culture are the values chosen by the senior leader, which dictate the behaviours expected throughout the company.

Values are not simply words written on a wall or included in a mission statement; they are living principles that must be modelled, reinforced, and upheld by everyone, starting with the CEO. A successful leader is both a **strategist** and a **cultural architect**, taking ownership of the values that shape how the organisation functions. In this chapter, we explore how selecting, embedding, and living these values can create a culture that drives performance, builds trust, and sustains success.

The Power of Choosing Values Wisely

Values are the foundation upon which culture is built. Choosing the right values to underpin your organisational culture is one of the most significant decisions a senior leader will make, in any organisation. It's not about selecting a laundry list of aspirational terms or values but about identifying a few (ideally no more than three to five) that truly resonate with the organisation's mission and strategic goals.

Why Focus on Only a Few Values?

When a leader chooses too many values, the impact is diluted. Employees struggle to remember, let alone live out, a long list of expectations. Focusing on just a few allows for depth rather than breadth, creating clarity around what truly matters. Moreover, it enables the organisation to monitor, measure, and hold people accountable for living those values daily.

For example, companies like Patagonia have become synonymous with values such as sustainability and transparency. They don't have a dozen values, just a handful that align directly with their mission to protect the planet while creating high quality outdoor gear. By narrowing their focus, they ensure every decision reflects those values.

The senior leader's task is to identify values that will serve as a compass for every action and decision in the company. But values alone won't create culture; it's the behaviours that bring them to life.

Defining Values Through Behaviour

One of the most common mistakes in organisational leadership is failing to clarify how values translate into behaviours. Values must be actionable and visible in everyday conduct. The process starts with defining specific, observable behaviours that reflect each value. Here's how a leader can do that:

1. **Choose a value**: Let's take the example of **Integrity**.
2. **Define the behaviours that support it**: What does integrity look like in practice? For senior leadership, it could involve transparent communication about both successes and challenges. For employees, it could mean being honest about mistakes and learning from them rather than covering them up.

By focusing on behaviours, leaders make it easier for employees to understand how to live the values in their day-to-day work. Let's explore how this works with some commonly chosen organisation values:

Integrity

- **Senior leadership**: Communicate openly and honestly about organisational challenges. Take ownership of mistakes and hold others accountable for doing the same.
- **Employees**: Be honest in all interactions, avoid cutting corners, and own up to errors without fear of reprisal.

Collaboration

- **Senior leadership:** Foster cross-functional teamwork by breaking down silos and encouraging knowledge sharing.

- **Employees**: Actively support colleagues, share resources, and offer help when needed, regardless of role or department.

Accountability

- **Senior leadership**: Set clear goals, follow through on commitments, and openly discuss setbacks.
- **Employees**: Take responsibility for personal performance, own up to mistakes, and seek solutions rather than blame others.

Each value must be reinforced by the leader's own behaviour, setting an example for others. If a leader espouses accountability but avoids taking responsibility for their own mistakes, the culture will be undermined. Actions always speak louder than words.

Culture as a Leadership Responsibility

The senior leader has two key responsibilities: **Culture and Strategy**. These are inseparable, as strategy outlines the destination while culture determines the journey. A leader who focuses solely on strategic goals without considering culture risks creating an environment where employees are disengaged, disconnected, or worse, actively working against the organisation's goals.

Expanding the Concept of Core Values and Their Impact

To truly embed values within an organisation, it's essential to understand how these values not only influence individual behaviour but also shape the entire ecosystem of decision-making, accountability, and even external reputation. The right values act as a filter for all actions, ensuring alignment from top leadership down to every single employee. But these values must go beyond mere words on paper. They should serve as the cornerstone of every major decision, both in good times and when the organisation faces challenges.

For example, consider the core value of transparency. When an organisation claims transparency as a fundamental value, it must reflect in daily practices, whether it's in honest internal communications, the way it handles customer complaints, or how it shares company updates with shareholders. Leaders set the tone by practising openness in team meetings, sharing setbacks as well as successes, and providing a clear rationale for their decisions.

In a world where corporate scandals regularly surface due to a lack of value-driven leadership, companies that authentically embody their values can stand apart. A case in point is Patagonia, the outdoor clothing company, which has made environmental responsibility its hallmark value. Patagonia's commitment to the environment is not a marketing gimmick but a value that informs everything from its product design to its supply chain decisions. This kind of consistency is a powerful example of how values, when taken seriously, can permeate an organisation's culture and brand identity, making a profound and positive impact.

Bridging the Gap Between Stated Values and Actual Behaviour

However, it's crucial to acknowledge that a gap often exists between the values that organisations claim to uphold and the behaviours that are witnessed on the ground. The *intention-behaviour gap* is a well-documented psychological concept where individuals or groups express certain principles but fail to live them out. This gap can be damaging to trust and morale within the organisation. Therefore, bridging this gap is a key role of leadership.

One strategy is through the use of values-based decision-making frameworks. These frameworks help employees at all levels make decisions by referring back to the organisation's core values. When faced with a difficult situation, asking questions like, 'Which option aligns most with our value of integrity?' can guide behaviour and keep everyone accountable to the agreed-upon principles.

Values in Action:

To solidify the role of values within a culture, look at how Zappos developed a robust organisational culture by infusing its core value of customer obsession. Zappos empowers its employees to go to extraordinary lengths to satisfy customer needs without the usual rigid protocols found in other customer service settings. This flexibility demonstrates that Zappos' leadership trusts its employees to make decisions that reflect the company's customer first philosophy, showing how values influence decision-making and operational flexibility.

Another powerful case is Unilever, whose commitment to sustainability has become embedded across its global operations. CEO Paul Polman famously scrapped quarterly reporting to move the company's focus to long-term sustainable growth, which better aligned with Unilever's core value of sustainability. In doing so, Unilever demonstrated that values can drive both operational processes and strategic decisions, thus shaping a culture where employees at all levels feel connected to a larger purpose.

Evaluating the Effectiveness of Values

Leadership also needs to actively measure whether the chosen values are being lived throughout the organisation. This is often done through employee engagement surveys, 360-degree feedback, and even customer feedback mechanisms. These tools help to assess whether the values are being upheld, not just in formal settings but in day-to-day operations. The results can highlight areas where there is a disconnect between values and behaviour, enabling leaders to intervene appropriately.

Reinforcing values requires not only communication but also recognition systems. A powerful way to integrate values into everyday actions is by rewarding employees who exemplify them. Publicly recognising those who go above and beyond to act in line with the organisation's values sends a clear message that such behaviour is not only expected but also appreciated and rewarded. Over time, this helps to deeply embed the desired values into the organisational culture.

The Senior Leader's Role in Living the Values

While values are often defined collectively by leadership teams, the senior leader has an irreplaceable role in ensuring that these values resonate throughout the organisation. They must serve as the chief role model, constantly reflecting on how their decisions, behaviours, and communication either reinforce or undermine the values they champion. It's important for senior leaders to consistently model the values to prevent the 'say-do' gap, where employees perceive leadership as disconnected from the company's stated values.

In summary, when values are carefully chosen, clearly defined, and embedded into every facet of the organisation, they become a powerful driver of both individual and organisational performance. The senior leader plays a pivotal role in setting this tone, creating a culture where the chosen values serve as the foundation for sustainable success.

Leaders Must Own the Culture

While a leader can solicit help from HR teams, consultants, or other experts in culture change, they can never abdicate responsibility for culture. It is not an HR initiative or a one-off project. It is a continuous process that requires leadership from the very top. The most successful cultures are leader-led. Employees look to their leaders to see how they should act, what behaviours are rewarded, and what values truly matter.

Take the example of Satya Nadella, CEO of Microsoft. When Nadella took over in 2014, Microsoft was seen as a bureaucratic and stagnant organisation. Nadella immediately set about reshaping the company's culture, focusing on values like **empathy** and a **growth mindset**. By consistently reinforcing these values in his own behaviour and decision-making, he transformed

Microsoft into one of the most innovative and high-performing companies in the world.

In contrast, the Post Office scandal in the UK highlights the consequences of a failure in cultural leadership. Hundreds of sub-postmasters were wrongly prosecuted for fraud due to a faulty IT system. Despite evidence emerging over many years, the culture of the organisation – one of fear and control – prevented senior leaders from acknowledging mistakes and addressing the issue. The CEO failed to drive the necessary cultural change, leading to a tragic failure in leadership and accountability.

Embedding Culture to Support Strategy

The right culture supports the achievement of strategic objectives, and the wrong culture can derail even the best laid plans. A culture that encourages openness, collaboration, and innovation allows employees to perform at their best, which in turn drives the sustainable achievement of the organisation's goals.

To do this, leaders need to actively embed the values and resulting behaviours into every aspect of the organisation. This can be achieved through several key practices:

1. **Recruitment:** Hire people who not only have the right skills but also align with the company's values. During the interview process, focus on whether candidates demonstrate behaviours that match your organisation's values.
2. **Onboarding and Training:** Incorporate the company's values into the onboarding process.

Ensure new employees understand how those values influence day-to-day behaviours and decisions.

3. **Performance Management**: Align performance metrics with values-based behaviours. Reward and recognise those who exemplify the organisation's values and ensure accountability for those who do not.

4. **Leadership Development**: Equip managers and leaders throughout the organisation with the tools to model and reinforce the values. Leadership must cascade the culture downwards, creating a consistent experience across all levels.

By embedding the culture in these areas, the senior leader ensures that the values are not just aspirational but are lived out across the entire organisation.

The Strategic Role of Values in Driving Business Outcomes

Values are not just abstract principles; they are the core foundation that drives decision-making, shapes behaviours, and directly influences organisational outcomes. When senior leaders clearly define and embed values into the organisational fabric, those values guide both strategic direction and everyday actions. For example, if a company adopts 'innovation' as a core value, this commitment should influence everything from hiring practices to resource allocation and product development.

Research shows that companies with clearly articulated values tend to outperform those without a strong value-based culture. A *Harvard Business Review* study found that organisations with strong, values-driven cultures are better equipped to weather economic downturns and achieve sustained performance. This is because values help employees understand what is expected of them, which in turn increases accountability and consistency in performance.

Patagonia's Values-Driven Business

A clear example of a company that uses its values as a strategic driver is Patagonia, an outdoor apparel brand. Patagonia's core value of environmental sustainability drives both its business strategy and its daily operations. The company famously ran an ad during Black Friday with the message 'Don't Buy This Jacket', urging consumers to reduce waste and think critically about consumption. Patagonia's values around sustainability are not just marketing gimmicks, they influence product design, materials used, and even how employees are expected to approach their work. This commitment has built a loyal customer base and set Patagonia apart as a company that stays true to its values while driving profitability.

Translating Values into Everyday Behaviours

For values to have real impact, they need to be translated into specific, observable behaviours. Leaders must ask themselves, 'What does it look like to live these values day-to-day?' Defining these behaviours creates clarity and helps align actions with the stated culture.

For example, if **integrity** is a chosen value, what does integrity look like in practice? It might mean being transparent with customers, openly admitting mistakes, or ensuring that the company's products meet the highest quality standards. If the value is **collaboration**, this could translate into expectations such as actively seeking diverse opinions during meetings, offering support to colleagues, and working together across departments to solve complex problems.

Creating Behavioural Guidelines

Many organisations choose to create behavioural guidelines to reinforce how values translate into practice. These guidelines outline specific actions and standards that employees are expected to follow. For instance, Google includes 'Respect the User' as a guiding principle, ensuring that every decision taken, from design to engineering, centres on user experience. These behaviours are ingrained across the organisation to ensure the value is not just an aspirational statement but a practical reality.

The Role of Senior Leadership in Reinforcing Values

Senior leaders play a crucial role in reinforcing organisational values. When leaders visibly live the values themselves, they create an environment where others feel compelled to follow. Employees take cues from the top, so if leaders consistently act in accordance with the chosen values, it sends a strong message across the organisation. On the other hand, any disconnect between leadership behaviour and the organisation's stated values can breed cynicism and mistrust, undermining the culture altogether.

This is particularly important during moments of crisis or challenge. Johnson & Johnson's handling of the Tylenol crisis in 1982 is a well-known example of how leadership aligned with values can preserve trust and integrity, even in the face of potential disaster. After several bottles of Tylenol were found to have been tampered with, resulting in fatalities, Johnson & Johnson quickly recalled millions of bottles, even though this led to a significant financial loss. The decision aligned with the company's long-standing value of putting customer safety first, and the company's transparent handling of the crisis preserved its reputation in the long run.

Communicating and Embedding Values Across the Organisation

A critical challenge for senior leaders is ensuring that organisational values resonate with employees at every level. This is particularly true in global organisations where different geographies and cultures may interpret values differently. Effective communication strategies need to be multi-faceted and continuous, not just a one-time announcement. Values need to be embedded in recruitment processes, performance reviews, and day-to-day management to ensure alignment across the board.

Use of Storytelling to Reinforce Values

One effective way to communicate values is through storytelling. Leaders can use real life examples from within the organisation to illustrate how values have been lived out, which helps employees connect with the values on a deeper, more personal level. For instance, Starbucks frequently highlights stories of employees going the extra mile for customers as a way to reinforce its value of customer service. Sharing these stories across the company can motivate employees to live the values themselves and foster a sense of pride in the organisation's culture.

The Danger of Misalignment: Values vs. Reality

When there is a mismatch between the organisation's stated values and actual behaviour, it can lead to significant issues. Employees may become disengaged, customers may lose trust, and in severe cases the company may face reputational damage. Misalignment can occur if values are not clearly communicated, or if there is inconsistent behaviour from leadership.

One well known example of value misalignment comes from Wells Fargo. The bank promoted the value of 'customer first' yet incentivised aggressive sales targets that pressured employees to open millions of fraudulent accounts. The stark gap between stated values and actual practices led to a massive scandal, legal penalties, and a dramatic loss of customer trust. This shows that a strong value system is only effective when the behaviours throughout the organisation genuinely reflect those values.

Conclusion: Leading with Values

In this chapter, we've explored the crucial role that values play in shaping an organisation's culture.

The senior leader must take full responsibility for defining, living, and embedding values that support both the people within the organisation and its strategic goals. By focusing on clear, observable behaviours and ensuring that values permeate every level of the organisation, leaders create a culture that drives sustainable performance and success.

Reflection: Questions for Leaders

As a senior leader, it's important to regularly reflect on the culture you are shaping. Here are a few questions to consider as you define and embed your organisation's values:

- What values matter most to me, how will they get the very best out of everyone, and how do they align with the organisation's mission and strategy?
- What specific behaviours reflect these values, and how am I modelling them?
- How am I reinforcing the culture through hiring, training, and performance management?
- How do I address behaviours that undermine the culture I want to build?
- Am I as intentional about culture as I am about strategy?

Chapter 3

United We Stand – The Power of Leadership Alignment

Introduction: The Leadership Alignment Imperative

When it comes to building and embedding an organisational culture, the senior leader and their leadership team play a critical role. It's not enough for the CEO or a few key individuals to be clear on the values that drive the organisation's success. Every leader in the senior team must be fully aligned with the chosen values and committed to demonstrating the agreed behaviours. Any cracks in this alignment can quickly cascade through the rest of the organisation, undermining the entire cultural framework.

The Cost of Misalignment at the Top

Leadership misalignment creates confusion and breeds mistrust. When senior leaders are not on the same page, employees quickly pick up on these signals. They notice conflicting messages, inconsistent priorities, and varying interpretations of the company's values. Misalignment in the senior team not only creates confusion, but it also stalls progress. Teams become paralysed by indecision, employees disengage, and the culture becomes fragmented. Without clear, unified leadership, you simply cannot expect the rest of the organisation to follow suit.

Uber's Internal Struggles

An example of leadership misalignment can be seen in Uber's earlier years. Despite strong values such as innovation and disruption, key leadership figures often operated in conflict. Former CEO Travis Kalanick's aggressive style of leadership clashed with other executives who questioned the ethical implications of some practices. This fractured approach created a toxic work culture, with differing behavioural norms tolerated across different parts of the organisation.

Why Alignment Matters: Building Trust and Credibility

When leadership is aligned, they send a clear and unified message to the rest of the organisation. This alignment serves two essential purposes:

1. **Trust:** Employees trust that decisions made by leadership are coherent and follow a shared vision.
2. **Credibility:** When leaders consistently live out the agreed behaviours, they reinforce the values they've communicated to their teams.

In contrast, when leadership is inconsistent, employees experience mixed signals, leading to confusion, disengagement, and frustration. For example, one leader might emphasise a value such as innovation, while another penalises employees for taking risks. This kind of misalignment can erode trust and credibility at every level of the organisation.

Flushing Out Disagreements: An Honest Dialogue Among Leaders

It is inevitable that even the best leadership teams will have different perspectives. However, disagreements over values or behaviours need to be addressed and resolved openly and early. Leaders cannot afford to work around these differences or pretend they don't exist. When it comes to culture, unresolved conflicts at the top can lead to inconsistent messaging that confuses employees.

Leadership Alignment as a Non-Negotiable for Organisational Success

Leadership alignment is not a luxury or an afterthought; it is the foundation upon which organisational success is built. Misalignment within the senior leadership team creates cracks that can lead to breakdowns in communication, inconsistency in decision-making, and confusion among employees. As business management expert Patrick Lencioni famously said, 'The single greatest advantage any company can achieve is organisational health.' And the health of any organisation begins with its leadership team.

In a study by McKinsey, it was found that companies with aligned leadership teams are more than twice as likely to outperform their competitors. The reasoning is simple: when leaders are aligned around a shared vision and values, they send consistent messages, make better decisions, and foster an environment where the entire organisation pulls in the same direction.

Practical Steps to Achieve Leadership Alignment

1. **Regular, Open Dialogue:** One of the critical elements of leadership alignment is continuous, open communication. Leaders should meet regularly to discuss strategic priorities, cultural objectives, and operational challenges. These conversations should encourage transparency, where leaders can voice concerns over misalignments without fear of judgment. Creating a psychologically safe environment where every leader feels comfortable raising difficult issues is vital for long-term alignment.

2. **Clarifying Roles and Responsibilities:** Misalignment often occurs when roles are unclear, leading to overlapping duties or gaps in accountability. The senior leadership team must have clearly defined roles that complement each other, ensuring that everyone knows where they stand and what is expected of them. Role clarity helps prevent conflicting directions from different leaders, which can confuse employees and dilute the culture.

3. **Alignment with Strategic Vision:** Senior leaders must continuously check whether they are all aligned with the company's overarching strategic vision. Without a shared understanding of where the organisation is headed, it is impossible to

consistently communicate values and expectations to employees. Leaders must periodically revisit and reaffirm their commitment to both the strategic direction and the organisational values, adjusting as necessary to maintain unity.

The Ripple Effect of Leadership Misalignment

When senior leadership is not aligned, it sends ripples of confusion and discord throughout the organisation. This can be particularly damaging when leaders are visibly at odds with one another, as it erodes trust among employees and can create competing priorities across departments. For example, if one leader promotes a customer-centric approach while another prioritises cost cutting, employees receive mixed signals, leading to paralysis or conflicting actions.

A high-profile case of leadership misalignment occurred at Uber under the leadership of its former CEO, Travis Kalanick. Conflicting leadership styles and values within the executive team, paired with a lack of unity around the company's culture, led to numerous scandals, including allegations of toxic work environments and unethical practices. The lack of alignment at the top had disastrous consequences, resulting in reputational damage and significant leadership turnover.

Creating a Shared Purpose

Leadership alignment also extends to a shared sense of purpose. It is not enough for leaders to simply agree on values; they must all have a deep, emotional connection to the company's mission and the behaviours that embody it. A lack of shared purpose can lead to superficial alignment, where leaders go through the motions of agreement but are not fully committed. This often leads to passive resistance or quiet disengagement from some members of the leadership team.

A tool that has proven effective in fostering shared purpose is the Visioning Workshop, where senior leaders come together to align not only on values but also on the company's purpose and long-term goals. These workshops often result in personal 'vision statements' from each leader, ensuring that everyone is fully bought into the mission, both intellectually and emotionally.

The Role of Emotional Intelligence in Leadership Alignment

In order for leaders to align effectively, they must also cultivate a high level of emotional intelligence (EI). Leaders with high EI are more self-aware and better equipped to constructively manage conflicts, leading to deeper alignment. A study from TalentSmart found that emotional intelligence is the strongest predictor of performance in the workplace, and it is particularly important for leaders who are striving for unity.

Emotional intelligence enables leaders to listen actively, understand differing perspectives, and foster a culture of empathy and collaboration. This helps avoid the 'echo chamber' effect, where leaders only surround themselves with like-minded people and ignore dissenting voices. Instead, emotionally intelligent leaders build alignment by encouraging healthy debate while guiding the team toward consensus.

The Importance of Self-Awareness

A key element in fostering leadership alignment is the ability of the senior leadership team to cultivate self-awareness and emotional intelligence. Each leader must not only have clarity about their own values and behaviours but also be attuned to how their actions impact others within the organisation. Emotional intelligence involves being able to navigate complex interpersonal dynamics, to understand how one's leadership style affects team morale, and to be adaptable in managing various personalities within the leadership team.

It's crucial that leaders engage in honest reflection and be willing to receive feedback. This, however, is often easier said than done. Leaders at the top may become isolated, making it difficult to get authentic feedback. Therefore, creating a system where feedback is encouraged and valued is vital. Leaders who are emotionally intelligent will model the behaviours they want to see from their teams, setting the tone for openness, honesty, and mutual respect.

Communication as the Backbone of Alignment

Alignment isn't just about agreeing on values. It's about consistently communicating those values in a way that resonates with the rest of the organisation. One of the most common reasons for misalignment at the top is a breakdown in communication. Even when leaders share a commitment to the same values, if they are not communicating them effectively or consistently, the message can become diluted or misinterpreted by their teams.

Establishing a culture of communication starts with senior leaders. Open, regular dialogue should be encouraged, not just during formal meetings but in everyday interactions. Leaders should take the time to ensure that everyone is on the same page regarding the interpretation of values and the corresponding behaviours. Tools such as structured communication frameworks or shared leadership meetings can help with this.

Another critical element is the ability to create 'safe spaces' where leadership teams can voice concerns or disagreements without fear of judgment. The sooner conflicts or differing viewpoints are addressed, the easier it becomes to resolve them in a constructive manner, strengthening the overall alignment.

Tangible Consequences of Misalignment

When senior leadership is misaligned, the entire organisation suffers. Misalignment at the top cascades downwards, leading to confusion at all levels of the organisation. Mixed messages or inconsistencies in leadership behaviours lead to a lack of trust among employees, and over time this trust deficit becomes detrimental to organisational performance.

Imagine a scenario where two senior leaders endorse completely different behaviours in relation to the same value. For example, if one leader encourages risk taking while another punishes mistakes, employees will be left unsure of what is expected of them. This ambiguity ultimately results in a lack of accountability and ownership, as people feel demotivated to take any action for fear of potential repercussions.

Studies have shown that aligned leadership not only improves employee engagement but also boosts organisational performance. When there is a clear, unified message from the top, employees feel more confident in their roles, are more productive, and have higher levels of job satisfaction.

The Role of Leadership in Crisis

A true test of leadership alignment often comes during times of crisis. When the organisation faces unexpected challenges, whether internal or external, the leadership's ability to stay united can determine the organisation's resilience. Leaders must be able to rely on their shared values to navigate through crises. A united front, built on a foundation of mutual trust and clear communication, can help the organisation maintain stability, even in turbulent times.

For instance, during the COVID-19 pandemic, organisations with strong leadership alignment were better equipped to adapt to the rapid changes in work environments, maintain employee engagement, and ensure the continued delivery of services. Leaders who were in sync in their decision-making and communication were able to navigate through uncertainty with a clear and consistent message to their workforce, ultimately preserving the company culture and morale during challenging times.

Evolving Together: Leadership Alignment Over Time

It's important to remember that alignment isn't static. Organisations change, markets shift, and even leadership teams evolve over time. What may have been an agreed-upon value or behaviour a few years ago may need to be revisited as the organisation grows or as external circumstances shift. Leadership alignment must be continuously nurtured, and regular reflection sessions or alignment workshops can help leaders recalibrate their focus and keep their behaviours aligned with the values that define the organisation's culture.

A practical step for ensuring long-term alignment is to periodically revisit the core values and assess whether they are still relevant to the current organisational landscape. Senior leadership teams should also invest in regular development opportunities that focus on team dynamics, values alignment, and personal leadership growth.

Leadership Alignment During Times of Change

One of the most significant tests of leadership alignment comes during periods of organisational change, whether it's a major restructuring, a merger, or the introduction of new strategic initiatives. During these times, leadership alignment is more crucial than ever. Misalignment during change can cause widespread confusion, resistance, and loss of morale.

Take the case of Ford Motor Company during the tenure of former CEO Alan Mulally. When Mulally took over, Ford was struggling with fragmented leadership and competing priorities within the organisation. He focused heavily on creating alignment among the senior team by instituting a weekly meeting called the Business Plan Review (BPR). This meeting brought all key leaders together to discuss progress, challenges, and priorities, in a transparent and collaborative way. Over time, this process helped align the leadership team and enabled Ford to successfully navigate its turnaround.

Unified Leadership as a Role Model for the Rest of the Organisation

When leaders are aligned, they serve as role models for the rest of the organisation. Employees observe leadership behaviour closely and take cues from how senior executives interact with one another. A unified leadership team sends a message of coherence, stability, and shared purpose, creating a trickledown effect that promotes organisational harmony.

However, if employees sense division or inconsistency among the leadership team, it can lead to confusion, anxiety, and a lack of trust in the leadership's direction. This phenomenon, known as 'leadership leakage', occurs when mixed messages from the top dilute the power of the values and behaviours the organisation is trying to instil.

Creating Space for Healthy Debate

Leadership alignment doesn't mean suppressing differing viewpoints. In fact, creating space for honest, productive dialogue is key to ensuring every voice in the leadership team is heard. Healthy debate allows senior leaders to surface any disagreements or concerns around the organisation's values or behaviours. However, this debate must ultimately lead to consensus. The role of the CEO in this process is crucial, not only in facilitating these discussions but also in ensuring that once the team aligns, everyone moves forward with full commitment.

The Non-Negotiables: Aligning on Values and Behaviours

For a leadership team to move forward, they must be absolutely clear on two things:

1. The **core values** that will guide the organisation.
2. The **specific behaviours** that embody those values.

A leadership team cannot afford ambiguity in either area. Once the core values are chosen, it's critical that every leader not only agrees with them but is also ready to live them out consistently. Similarly, leaders must be explicit about what these values look like in terms of day-to-day behaviours. The best way to make this clear is to co-create behaviour guidelines that serve as touchstones for decision-making, interactions, and strategic actions across the company.

Example: Integrity as a Core Value

Let's say the senior leadership team chooses **integrity** as a core value. What does this mean for day-to-day behaviour? It's not enough to declare that integrity matters; leaders must show how it translates into specific actions. For instance:

- Always telling the truth, even when it's difficult.
- Transparency in communication, especially when addressing challenges or failures.
- Holding everyone accountable to the same standards, regardless of seniority or position.

Every leader must demonstrate these behaviours consistently to avoid confusion and double standards. It's this consistency that solidifies trust and brings the organisation closer together around its shared values.

Behavioural Consistency: The Key to Embedding Culture

One of the biggest threats to organisational culture is when leaders fail to model the behaviours they preach. Leaders need to be mindful that their actions, no matter how small, are under constant observation. If a leader says that collaboration is key but operates in a siloed manner, it sends a clear message to employees that the stated values don't really matter.

The Ripple Effect of Leadership Behaviour

The behaviour of senior leaders cascades down through the ranks. When leaders consistently live out the agreed behaviours, it sets the tone for the entire organisation. This is the ripple effect; when leaders model the right behaviours, employees take note and follow suit.

Inconsistencies, on the other hand, cause confusion. For example, if a company values **teamwork** but some leaders only reward individual achievements, employees will quickly learn that the stated value is not a real priority. This inconsistency causes frustration and disengagement, eroding the culture from within.

The CEO's Role in Maintaining Alignment

While alignment is the responsibility of the entire senior team, the CEO plays a particularly crucial role in ensuring the team stays united. As the chief cultural architect, the CEO must not only live the values but also create an environment where alignment is nurtured and maintained. This means:

- Holding regular check-ins with the senior team to assess how well they are living out the values.
- Being open to feedback and course corrections.
- Ensuring that any new hires at the senior level are aligned with the organisation's cultural values from day one.

Pitfalls to Avoid: The Dangers of Superficial Agreement

One of the biggest dangers in leadership teams is superficial agreement. This occurs when leaders outwardly agree with decisions and values but inwardly harbour doubts or disagreements. Over time, these unspoken reservations can grow into larger issues that undermine the team's unity.

Creating Psychological Safety

To avoid superficial agreement, the leadership team must cultivate an environment of psychological safety, where each member feels comfortable expressing concerns and offering dissenting views without fear of retribution. When leaders feel safe to voice differing opinions, the organisation benefits from a more robust decision-making process, and the likelihood of alignment increases.

The Consequences of Failing to Align

A failure to align at the senior level can have far-reaching consequences. The Post Office scandal, discussed earlier, is an example of how a lack of alignment in values and behaviours among leadership led to a disastrous outcome. While some senior leaders were aware of the cultural issues and concerns raised by employees, others chose to ignore them, resulting in a massive breakdown in trust and integrity.

Misalignment can also manifest in more subtle ways, such as high turnover among senior leaders, disjointed strategy implementation, or inconsistent communication. These issues may not be immediately obvious, but over time they erode the organisation's performance and culture.

How to Achieve and Maintain Alignment

Achieving and maintaining alignment requires ongoing effort. Some strategies include:

- **Regular Cultural Check-Ins:** The senior team should regularly assess how well they are living the values and exhibiting the agreed-upon behaviours.
- **Honest Feedback Loops:** Leaders must create feedback loops where they can openly discuss challenges or areas where they may not be fully aligned.
- **Collective Accountability:** The senior team must hold each other accountable for staying aligned with the culture. This means calling out misaligned behaviours and course-correcting as needed.

Conclusion: United We Stand

Leadership alignment is not a one-time event. It is an ongoing commitment that requires vigilance, honesty, and a willingness to hold each other accountable. A senior team that is fully aligned on values and behaviours can create a powerful, cohesive culture that permeates every level of the organisation. However, without this alignment, the cultural framework will crumble, and any efforts to build a strong, sustainable culture will be in vain.

In the end, the alignment of the senior team sets the tone for the entire organisation. When leaders are united, employees feel confident in the direction of the organisation and trust that the culture is being built on a solid foundation.

Reflection: Questions for Leaders

To ensure alignment within your senior leadership team, ask yourself:

- Are we all clear on the core values and the specific behaviours that reflect those values?
- Do we have open, honest conversations about any misalignment?
- How consistently are we modelling the values we've agreed upon?
- How are we holding each other accountable for living the culture we want to create?

Chapter 4

Spreading the Message – Crafting a Communication Strategy to Embed the Desired Culture

Introduction: The Power of Communication in Cultural Transformation

An organisation's culture is only as strong as its communication. Even the most well-defined values and behaviours will fail to take root if not communicated effectively. A robust communication strategy is essential for ensuring that everyone, from senior leaders to the newest employee, understands and embodies the chosen values and behaviours. Whether your organisation consists of 50 people or 50,000 spread across different continents, communication is the bridge that connects leadership's cultural vision to daily practices.

In this chapter, we will explore how to craft a communication strategy that works for both small and large organisations, addressing the unique challenges of different organisational sizes, structures, and geographies.

Tailoring the Message: Adapting Communication to Audience and Context

The key to a successful communication strategy is adapting your message to your audience. The values and behaviours that you aim to embed must be communicated in a way that resonates with everyone in the organisation, regardless of their role, location, or level of seniority.

- **For small organisations**: In organisations with fewer than 100 employees, communication can be more personal. Leaders may be able to deliver the message directly in meetings or through one-on-one conversations. The advantage here is the potential for more intimate, direct dialogue, which builds trust and ensures the message is heard.

- **For larger organisations**: Scaling the communication becomes more challenging with thousands of employees across multiple locations. In these cases, leveraging technology and cascading communication through layers of leadership becomes critical. However, the message must remain consistent, no matter how many channels it goes through.

Key Considerations for Both Sizes:

- **Clarity**: Ensure that the values and behaviours are communicated in simple, relatable terms. Avoid jargon or abstract concepts that can confuse the message.

- **Relevance**: Employees need to see how the values and behaviours connect to their daily work. Tailor examples to different departments or locations to make the message relevant.

The Role of Leadership: Leading from the Front in Communication

The most effective communication strategy starts at the top. The CEO and senior leadership team must be the first to embody and communicate the chosen values and behaviours. This is especially important for embedding culture, because employees will take their cues from how leaders behave, not just from what they say.

Ways Leadership Can Drive Communication:

- **Visible and consistent presence**: Whether in person, through video messages, or town hall meetings, leaders must be visible and vocal about the organisation's values and resulting behaviours. For instance, in large global organisations, video messages from the CEO can ensure a consistent message reaches everyone, no matter where they are based.
- **Storytelling**: Leaders can make values and behaviours come alive by sharing stories of how these values have influenced business decisions, customer interactions, or internal operations. Personal stories resonate far more than generic memos.
- **Walking the talk**: Employees will quickly pick up on any discrepancies between the message and leaders' actions. It's crucial that senior leaders model the behaviours they want to see across the organisation, reinforcing their importance.

Digital Communication as a Culture-Building Tool

In today's global and often remote work environments, digital communication has become a crucial component in embedding organisational culture. Whether your organisation operates with teams in one office or across several countries, leveraging digital platforms to consistently communicate the company's values and behaviours is vital. Tools such as Slack, Microsoft Teams, or dedicated intranet portals, allow for continuous engagement and dialogue, ensuring that the organisation's message reaches all employees, no matter their location.

Organisations with a dispersed workforce can set up regular virtual town halls or Q&A sessions, led by senior leadership, to reinforce cultural messages. These platforms also allow for transparency; employees can see how leaders are embodying the values themselves, fostering trust. According to a study by Gartner, organisations that successfully employ digital communication strategies see a 15% increase in employee engagement and cultural alignment.

For example, at Buffer – a fully remote company – digital tools play a key role in embedding the company's core values. Every employee has access to public channels where senior leadership regularly shares updates, celebrates behaviours aligned with the company's values, and answers questions in real time. This continuous interaction not only reinforces the company's culture but also builds a sense of inclusivity and shared purpose among remote teams.

Overcoming Resistance Through Clear Communication

In any organisation, especially larger or geographically dispersed ones, there may be resistance to cultural change. It's not uncommon for employees to feel attached to the previous way of doing things or to question whether the new values will genuinely impact their day-to-day work. Addressing resistance early and directly is vital.

A good communication strategy doesn't just deliver the 'what' and 'how' of cultural changes but also clearly articulates the 'why'. When employees understand why certain values are chosen and how these changes benefit them individually and collectively, resistance tends to diminish. Case studies or examples from other departments or organisations that have successfully implemented similar values can also be powerful tools in convincing hesitant employees.

Consistency in Messaging: Aligning Words with Actions

An important element of a communication strategy is ensuring consistency between what the leadership communicates and what the employees experience on the ground. Employees quickly notice when the values being broadcasted by leadership don't align with everyday practices. Therefore, leaders must not only communicate values clearly but also model the behaviours that reflect those values.

For example, if 'integrity' is one of the core values, the leadership team should be transparent in their communication, especially in difficult situations. This could mean being upfront about business challenges, sharing honest updates, and taking accountability when things go wrong. Employees will be more likely to adopt the values if they see their leaders embodying them consistently.

Celebrating Milestones in the Cultural Journey

Celebrating progress is an essential part of reinforcing the culture. As the communication strategy rolls out and starts to take effect, acknowledge the milestones. Whether it's recognising teams that have effectively embraced the new values or celebrating individuals who have gone above and beyond in living the company's values, these celebrations serve to reinforce the message.

Public recognition, whether through internal newsletters, town hall meetings, or social media, acts as a powerful motivator. It communicates to the entire organisation that the cultural transformation is being taken seriously and that those who align with the values will be recognised and rewarded.

Leadership Visibility and Role-Modelling

Leadership visibility is another critical component of embedding the desired culture. When senior leaders are consistently seen, heard, and understood by all employees, it sends a powerful message of commitment to the company's cultural goals. But it's not just about being seen, it's about being seen to live the values. The most effective communicators are those who role model the behaviours they are trying to embed.

Leaders should aim to incorporate cultural messaging into every major communication, from strategic updates to quarterly reviews. They should also attend departmental meetings, host informal coffee sessions, or participate in employee roundtables. These interactions provide leaders with the opportunity to reinforce values, listen to employee concerns, and demonstrate how the desired behaviours are being embodied at all levels.

At Southwest Airlines, the CEO regularly participates in frontline activities and employee meetings to reinforce the company's core value of customer service excellence. This high level of visibility demonstrates leadership commitment to the culture and encourages employees to embody the same values in their day-to-day work. Over time, these actions create a trickledown effect, where employees begin to replicate the desired behaviours, knowing that their leaders are living the values.

Tailoring the Message to Different Audiences

A communication strategy to embed organisational culture must be adaptable to different audiences within the company. Not all employees will resonate with the same messaging, so it is important to tailor your approach based on departments, functions, or even geographic regions. This customisation ensures that the core message remains consistent but speaks to the unique challenges or motivations of each group.

For example, frontline employees may need messaging that is more operationally focused: what do the company's values mean for their day-to-day interactions with customers? In contrast, senior managers might require a more strategic lens: how do these values drive decision-making, leadership style, and long-term objectives?

Cultural communication should be made relevant to the local context, especially in global organisations. What works in one region may need to be adapted for another, while still maintaining the integrity of the overarching message. Take the global communication strategies of Unilever, which maintains a consistent company culture while tailoring the language and examples of their core values to fit different cultural contexts across their global workforce. This balance allows for both global cohesion and local relevance.

Creating Feedback Loops to Measure Effectiveness

Effective communication is a two-way street. While leaders need to broadcast the company's values and behaviours clearly and consistently, it's equally important to ensure that there are mechanisms in place to capture employee feedback on these messages. Feedback loops, such as employee surveys, focus groups, or suggestion boxes, allow organisations to gauge how well the culture is being understood and embedded.

These mechanisms also give employees a voice, fostering a culture of inclusivity and transparency. Employees who feel heard and see their feedback acted upon are more likely to engage with and embody the company's values. According to Gallup, organisations that encourage employee feedback see a 14% increase in productivity and a 20% increase in profitability.

By implementing regular feedback channels, you ensure that the communication strategy is not a one-off initiative but an ongoing dialogue. For example, IBM uses regular pulse surveys to assess how well cultural messages are being received and whether employees feel connected to the company's core values. Leadership teams then act on this feedback, refining their communication efforts and making adjustments to improve cultural alignment.

Consistency and Repetition of Messaging

Repetition is key to embedding culture. Leaders should not assume that one communication will suffice. Instead, values, behaviours, and cultural expectations need to be communicated frequently, across multiple channels. Whether it's through newsletters, meetings, workshops, or digital updates, repetition reinforces the message and helps build a shared understanding.

For example, Zappos, known for its customer-centric culture, uses every opportunity to reinforce its core values. From onboarding programmes to weekly all-hands meetings, the company ensures that its values are woven into every aspect of communication. This constant reinforcement has enabled Zappos to maintain its strong culture despite rapid growth.

Choosing the Right Channels: Leveraging Multiple Platforms for Communication

Different organisations will require different communication channels, depending on size, structure, and geography. A robust communication strategy must consider the best platforms to ensure the message reaches everyone.

Communication Channels for Small Organisations:

- **Face-to-face meetings**: Small teams can gather for company-wide meetings or regular briefings to discuss values and behaviours. This provides opportunities for direct feedback and clarification.
- **Email and intranet**: In larger organisations, email or a company intranet can be effective for sharing updates, reminders, and reinforcing key messages.

Communication Channels for Large Organisations:

- **Company-wide town halls (virtual and in person)**: Regular town halls with the CEO or senior leadership team can address the entire organisation. Technology platforms like Zoom, Teams, or Webex allow for global participation.
- **Internal communication platforms**: Tools like Microsoft Teams, Slack, or Yammer can be leveraged to share updates, host discussions, and encourage feedback. These platforms also allow for the sharing of content such as videos, infographics, and case studies that reinforce the values.
- **Cascading communication through managers**: In large organisations, it's critical that the communication cascades through all levels of management. This means ensuring that middle managers fully understand and can communicate the values and behaviours to their teams. Providing managers with toolkits or talking points ensures consistency.

Embedding Communication in Everyday Operations: Reinforcing the Message

Once the values and behaviours have been communicated, the real challenge begins: ensuring that these principles are consistently reinforced in the day-to-day operations of the organisation. Communication cannot be a one-off event. It must be part of the organisational fabric.

Embedding in Processes:

- **Onboarding:** New employees should be introduced to the organisation's values and behaviours from day one. This ensures that they understand the expectations from the start. Integrating culture into onboarding processes, through workshops, training sessions, or mentorship programmes, helps embed the message early.
- **Performance reviews:** Include culture and behaviours as a formal part of performance reviews. Employees should be evaluated not just on what they achieve but on how they achieve it. This reinforces the idea that behaviours aligned with the values are just as important as outcomes.
- **Internal communications:** Regular newsletters, updates on the company intranet, or video messages from leaders should consistently refer to the values and behaviours. Recognition of employees who exemplify these values in their work can be a powerful tool for reinforcing the message.

Measuring the Impact: Gauging Understanding and Engagement

A successful communication strategy doesn't end with sending out messages. It's crucial to measure the impact of the communication and assess how well the values and behaviours are understood and adopted across the organisation.

Feedback Mechanisms:

- **Surveys and pulse checks:** Regular employee surveys can gauge how well the values are understood and whether employees feel that the behaviours are being modelled by leadership. Use short, frequent pulse checks to track engagement.
- **Focus groups:** Organise focus groups to dive deeper into how employees feel about the culture. These small group settings allow for more nuanced feedback and provide an opportunity for employees to express concerns or suggestions.
- **Open door policy:** Encouraging open dialogue between employees and leaders is vital for maintaining ongoing alignment. Employees should feel comfortable approaching managers with questions or feedback regarding the values and behaviours.

Addressing Global and Cultural Diversity in Communication

For organisations with a global presence, it's important to consider cultural differences in how values are perceived and understood. While the core message should remain the same, the method of communication may need to be adapted to fit different cultural contexts.

Cultural Sensitivity in Communication:

- **Localising the message**: While the core values remain the same, communication must respect cultural nuances. For example, in some cultures, direct feedback may be less acceptable, so the way behaviours like openness or collaboration are communicated may differ.
- **Multilingual support**: Ensure that key messages are translated accurately and delivered in the native language of all employees. This helps ensure that no-one feels excluded or misunderstood.
- **Regional leaders as cultural ambassadors**: In global organisations, regional leaders can act as ambassadors for the values, helping to contextualise the behaviours for different cultural environments while maintaining alignment with the organisation's overarching vision.

Sustaining the Communication Strategy Over Time

Embedding a culture is not a one-time event. The communication strategy must be sustained over the long term to ensure the values and behaviours become ingrained in the organisation's DNA.

Ongoing Communication:

- **Regular updates from leadership**: Periodic messages from the CEO or senior leaders, reinforcing the values, are essential. These updates can highlight milestones, share success stories, or acknowledge employees who are living the values.
- **Celebrating success**: Recognising and celebrating individuals or teams who exemplify the desired behaviours strengthens the culture. Employee awards, shout-outs in companywide meetings, or feature stories in newsletters, can serve as powerful reminders.
- **Adapting and evolving**: As the organisation grows and evolves, so too should the communication strategy. Regularly assess whether the chosen values and behaviours are still relevant and whether the communication methods are effective. Being open to feedback and adapting the strategy accordingly is key to long-term success.

Conclusion: Spreading the Message for Long-Term Cultural Success

Crafting and implementing an effective communication strategy is essential for embedding the values, behaviours, and culture within an organisation. Whether you're leading a small team or a global workforce, the principles remain the same: clarity, consistency, and sustained effort. By aligning the message across all levels of the organisation and using the right communication tools, leaders can create a shared understanding that drives the cultural transformation needed for long-term success.

Reflection: Questions for Leaders

To ensure your communication strategy effectively embeds your desired culture, ask yourself:

- Are we leveraging the right communication channels? Have we identified the most effective platforms to reach all employees, whether they're in one location or spread globally?
- How visible is our leadership in communicating culture? Are senior leaders consistently modelling and reinforcing the values in every interaction and message?
- Is our messaging tailored to different audiences? Have we adapted our cultural messaging to resonate with the diverse needs of various departments, regions, or teams?
- Are feedback loops in place? Do we have mechanisms, such as surveys or focus groups, which allow us to gauge how well the message is being received and understood?
- How consistent is our cultural communication? Are we repeating and reinforcing the values and behaviours regularly through multiple channels to ensure alignment and understanding?
- Are employees engaged in the communication process? Have we created opportunities for employees to voice their thoughts and feel part of the cultural conversation?

Chapter 5

The Power of Trust –
Build, Break, Rebuild

Introduction: Trust as the Cornerstone of Culture

Trust is the foundation upon which successful organisations are built. It shapes every interaction, decision, and relationship within an organisation, and it's critical for fostering collaboration, innovation, and engagement. Without trust, even the best strategies falter, and talented teams lose their potential. When trust is absent, organisations risk high employee turnover, disengagement, and a fractured culture.

In today's fast paced and often turbulent business environment, leaders must understand that trust is not a given; it is earned. Moreover, it is fragile. While building trust is a long and deliberate process, it can be broken in an instant. The ability of a leader to cultivate, maintain, and when necessary rebuild trust is one of the most critical factors determining an organisation's long-term success.

Trust plays a foundational role in creating and sustaining a healthy organisational culture. Trust is the glue that holds a team together, allowing open communication, collaboration, and innovation. When employees trust their leaders and peers, they are more likely to engage fully, align with the organisation's values, and exhibit the behaviours that reflect the desired culture. Conversely, when trust is broken, it can undermine the culture, leading to disengagement, fear, and resistance to change.

A culture of trust is essential for fostering an environment where individuals feel safe to take risks, admit mistakes, and grow. This is crucial for organisations aiming for long-term success, as trust allows for honest feedback and adaptability, which are vital in a rapidly changing business landscape. Leaders must actively build, maintain, and, when necessary, repair trust to ensure that the cultural values they have chosen do permeate every level of the organisation.

This chapter explores how trust is constructed, how it can be damaged or lost, and the deliberate steps needed to rebuild it. Trust is not just a 'nice-to-have' but a business imperative, particularly in modern, complex organisational environments where collaboration and agility are essential.

Building Trust: The Essential Ingredients

The Role of Leadership in Building Trust

Trust begins at the top. Senior leaders are the chief architects of trust in an organisation. Their behaviours, decisions, and communication styles set the tone for the entire workforce. When leaders behave in a trustworthy manner, they foster a culture of trust that permeates all levels of the organisation.

One of the key roles of leaders is to model the values and behaviours that the organisation claims to stand for. If integrity, for example, is a core value, leaders must demonstrate this in every decision they make. This consistency between stated values and actions helps build trust among employees, stakeholders, and customers alike.

Transparency: The Key to Unlocking Trust

Transparency is a powerful tool in trust-building. In any organisation, uncertainty breeds mistrust. When people don't know what's happening or why decisions are being made, they begin to speculate, often assuming the worst. This can erode trust even when there is no ill intent.

To foster transparency, leaders need to communicate openly about the challenges the organisation is facing, the rationale behind decisions, and the future direction of the company. This communication needs to be both top-down and bottom-up. Employees should feel they are not only informed but also heard. Transparency is not just about providing information but about ensuring that the information is clear, timely, and accessible.

In practical terms, transparency can be fostered through regular all-hands meetings, transparent decision-making processes, and clear communication around organisational changes. In a high trust organisation, transparency is not seen as a risk but as an opportunity to engage employees and stakeholders.

Consistency and Reliability: Trust's Silent Guardians

Trust thrives on consistency. If leaders say one thing and do another, trust will quickly erode. Consistency in communication, decision-making, and behaviour is crucial. This is where the concept of 'walking the talk' comes into play. Leaders must follow through on commitments and act in ways that align with the organisation's values.

Employees watch closely how leaders behave in high-pressure situations. If leaders abandon their values when times get tough, trust can be shattered. On the other hand, when leaders maintain consistency under pressure, trust deepens. Consistency builds a sense of reliability, which is essential for long-term trust.

For example, a leader who consistently supports flexible working arrangements, even when deadlines are looming, sends a strong message that they value work-life balance. This consistency builds trust in the leader's commitment to employee wellbeing.

Empathy and Listening: Trust Through Connection

Trust is also built through empathy and active listening. Leaders who listen to their employees, understand their concerns and act on them, are far more likely to build trust. Empathy involves putting oneself in another's shoes and considering how decisions will impact others. Leaders who can demonstrate empathy create stronger, more trusting relationships.

Active listening, particularly in conflict situations, is key to building trust. When employees feel that their voices are heard and their perspectives are valued, they are more likely to trust leadership decisions, even if they don't entirely agree with them.

Trust Is Hard to Build, Easy to Lose

Trust, while difficult to establish, can be lost in a moment. Whether it's through inconsistent communication, failure to follow through on promises, or ethical lapses, once trust is broken its impact reverberates through the entire organisation. This breakdown in trust can manifest in several ways, all of which significantly hinder an organisation's ability to function effectively.

The Fragility of Trust

Trust is a powerful yet delicate force within an organisation. It can take years to build, moments to break, and yet, with the right approach, it can be rebuilt stronger than ever. When trust exists between a leader and their team, it allows for openness, innovation, and the freedom to challenge and grow. Employees feel secure in their roles, they are more likely to take risks, voice concerns, and contribute meaningfully to the company's goals. Without trust, however, these same environments become rigid, fearful, and unproductive.

Trust is cumulative, built incrementally over time through consistent actions, transparent communication, and mutual respect. Leaders earn trust by showing their employees they have their best interests at heart, which means making decisions with the broader welfare of the team in mind.

But, as important as it is, leaders must remember that trust is not static. It is dynamic and can ebb and flow depending on circumstances, perceptions, and actions. This means leaders need to remain vigilant and committed to nurturing trust on an ongoing basis, especially in challenging times.

Trust and Psychological Safety

A critical component of trust is the concept of psychological safety, the belief that one will not be punished or humiliated for speaking up with ideas, questions, or concerns. Trust forms the foundation of psychological safety, allowing employees to feel comfortable enough to contribute without fear of judgment. When employees know their contributions are valued, even when they bring forward challenges or dissenting opinions, the entire organisation thrives.

This sense of safety is key for high performing teams. Google's famous 'Project Aristotle' identified psychological safety as the number one factor in team effectiveness. In organisations where trust is lacking, employees might remain silent when it matters most, which can result in missed opportunities, poor decision-making, and even ethical breaches.

A leader who prioritises trust-building creates an environment where employees feel empowered, knowing they can rely on both their peers and their leaders.

When Trust Breaks

The breakdown of trust can be sudden or gradual, stemming from a single event or a series of missteps. Often, trust erodes when leaders fail to follow through on promises, act in self-interest, or withhold information from their teams. This is particularly true when there is a misalignment between what leaders say and do. Inconsistency, in this regard, is the primary enemy of trust.

An important example can be drawn from organisational culture during times of change or crisis. When leaders implement sweeping changes without transparent communication, employee trust can be quickly undermined. Even if the change is for the benefit of the company, the manner in which it is introduced often dictates whether trust is sustained or broken. Employees who are caught off guard, or who feel left out of important decisions, begin to question their leaders' integrity and motives.

Trust can also falter when there is a perception of unfairness. When leaders are seen as playing favourites or making decisions that appear biased, employees begin to doubt their judgment and commitment to the group. This can fracture teams, leading to disengagement and, ultimately, higher turnover.

Rebuilding trust after a breach is no easy task, but it is possible. It requires humility, transparency, and a willingness to acknowledge mistakes. Leaders who have lost the trust of their teams must first listen, then take responsibility for their role in the breakdown.

Rebuilding Trust: A Leadership Imperative

Once trust is broken, the journey to rebuild it can be challenging, but leaders must view this as an opportunity to foster an even stronger connection with their teams. Rebuilding trust begins with open communication and honesty. This means not only addressing the specific incident that led to the breakdown but also making a renewed commitment to transparency and consistency moving forward.

A successful approach to rebuilding involves:

1. **Acknowledging the breach**: Leaders need to openly acknowledge the issue that led to the loss of trust. This involves taking full responsibility for their actions (or inactions) and resisting the temptation to deflect or make excuses.
2. **Empathy and understanding**: Leaders must actively listen to their employees, understanding the impact of the breach on both individuals and the collective team. Showing empathy during this stage helps to re-establish emotional connection.
3. **Actionable follow-through**: Words alone will not suffice. To rebuild trust, leaders must provide clear steps and actions they will take to prevent similar breaches in the future. These actions must align with the values of the organisation.
4. **Consistency and time**: Rebuilding trust is a long-term endeavour. Leaders must consistently demonstrate trustworthy behaviour over time, proving that their commitment to change is genuine.
5. **Fostering transparency**: Moving forward, leaders should prioritise transparency in all dealings. This means openly sharing the reasoning behind decisions, especially in difficult or uncertain times.

One of the most powerful elements of trust rebuilding is the fact that, once recovered, it often creates deeper bonds within teams. A team that has faced adversity together, worked through mistrust and come out the other side, is often more resilient, cohesive, and united than they were before the crisis.

Trust and Organisational Resilience

In an era marked by rapid change, uncertainty, and disruption, trust is more important than ever. Trust not only helps organisations navigate immediate challenges, but it also positions them for long-term success. It creates the conditions necessary for organisational resilience, the ability to adapt, survive, and thrive in the face of disruption.

Teams that trust one another can collaborate more effectively, innovate more boldly, and recover more quickly from setbacks. This resilience is crucial for organisations operating in competitive markets, where the ability to respond to change is often the difference between success and failure.

By making trust a core organisational value, leaders are investing in the long-term success and sustainability of their companies.

The Post Office Horizon IT Scandal: A Case of Broken Trust

A prime example of the catastrophic impact of broken trust can be seen in the Post Office Horizon IT scandal. Hundreds of sub-postmasters were wrongly accused of theft, fraud, and false accounting because of faulty software. These accusations, based on flawed data, resulted in financial ruin, legal battles, and even imprisonment for many. The scandal, caused by a lack of transparency and accountability, highlighted a complete failure in leadership and culture.

The trust between the Post Office and its sub-postmasters – key partners in its business model – was shattered. Rebuilding that trust has proven incredibly challenging, as the damage went far beyond the individuals involved and became a symbol of systemic failure. The public, employees, and partners lost faith in the institution, and the organisation's culture was seen as one that prioritised self-preservation over integrity and accountability.

The Post Office has since been working to repair the damage, but the scandal serves as a stark reminder that once trust is broken, it can take years, if not decades, to rebuild.

The Fallout of Broken Trust: Disengagement and Attrition

When trust is broken, one of the immediate consequences is a drop in employee engagement. Employees who feel that they can no longer trust their leaders, or the organisation, disengage from their work. They may become less productive, withhold discretionary effort or, in extreme cases, actively undermine the organisation.

Disengaged employees are more likely to leave the company, leading to higher turnover rates. High employee turnover is costly, both in terms of recruitment and the loss of institutional knowledge. Furthermore, it creates a vicious cycle where remaining employees become even more disengaged due to the churn around them.

Low trust can also lead to a breakdown in communication and collaboration. In a high trust organisation, people feel safe sharing ideas and giving feedback. When trust is lost, people are more likely to keep their thoughts to themselves, avoid difficult conversations, and work in silos.

Rebuilding Trust: A Long-Term Commitment

Step 1: Acknowledging Mistakes

The first step in rebuilding trust is acknowledging the mistake or breach of trust. This must be done openly and honestly. Leaders need to admit where they went wrong and demonstrate a genuine commitment to making things right. Often, this requires a public apology and a clear explanation of what went wrong and why.

Step 2: Taking Accountability

Merely acknowledging mistakes is not enough; leaders must take accountability for them. This means going beyond simply admitting fault. Leaders must outline the steps they will take to correct the issue and prevent it from happening again. Taking ownership of the problem signals to employees that leaders are serious about change.

For example, after the fallout from the Horizon IT scandal, the Post Office leadership had to take accountability not only for the wrongful accusations but also for the systemic issues that allowed the scandal to persist for so long. This included making reparations to those affected and committing to more transparent and accountable leadership practices.

Step 3: Consistent and Transparent Actions

Rebuilding trust is not a quick fix; it requires consistent effort over time. Leaders must follow through on their commitments and continue to act in ways that align with the organisation's values. Transparency, which is crucial for building trust, becomes even more critical in the rebuilding process. Leaders must over-communicate during this time, ensuring that employees know what steps are being taken and why.

For example, a leader may choose to implement more frequent check-ins with their teams, provide detailed updates on organisational changes, or open up new channels for employee feedback. These actions, sustained over time, will help to rebuild trust and show that leadership is committed to the long-term health of the organisation.

Step 4: Inviting Feedback and Learning From It

Leaders rebuilding trust must also be willing to listen to feedback from their employees and act on it. This means creating safe spaces where employees can voice their concerns without fear of retaliation. When employees feel heard, they are more likely to reengage with the organisation and its leadership.

Leadership, Trust, and Organisational Success

Trust as a Driver of High Performance

A culture of trust is directly linked to higher organisational performance. In a high-trust culture, employees are more engaged, more collaborative, and more willing to take risks. They are also more likely to bring forward ideas that can drive innovation. When trust is present, employees feel safe to fail, knowing that mistakes will be viewed as learning opportunities rather than failures.

Embedding Trust into Organisational Culture

For trust to truly permeate an organisation, it must be embedded in the culture. This requires intentionality from leaders. Trust-building practices, such as transparent communication, regular feedback loops, and consistent behaviour, must become part of the organisation's DNA. Leaders should also ensure that they are developing future leaders who understand the importance of trust and know how to build it.

Trust as the Cornerstone of High-Performing Teams

Building trust within an organisation is critical for high performance. Research consistently shows that trust is the foundation of collaboration, innovation, and engagement. According to a study by *Harvard Business Review*, employees in high-trust organisations report 50% higher productivity and 76% more engagement than their counterparts in low-trust environments. This isn't just about personal relationships but extends to organisational trust, confidence that the company's systems, processes, and leadership decisions align with its values.

Leaders play a crucial role in establishing this foundation. Trust must be demonstrated at the top to permeate through every level of the organisation. The most successful leaders foster an environment where open communication, transparency, and integrity are the norm. By modelling trustworthy behaviours, such as admitting mistakes, acting consistently, and being transparent about decisions, leaders set the tone for the entire company.

However, trust can be fragile. Leaders must acknowledge that trust can be broken through misaligned actions, broken promises, or a lack of transparency. Once broken, rebuilding trust requires a deliberate strategy, one that focuses on accountability, consistent behaviour, and an authentic commitment to rectifying mistakes.

Rebuilding Trust after Breakdowns

Even in the best-run organisations, trust can falter. The key is in how leaders handle these situations. When trust is broken, whether through failed promises, poor decision-making, or a lack of accountability, leaders must prioritise rebuilding it. This begins with acknowledging the breach. Avoiding or deflecting blame will only compound the issue, while transparency and vulnerability can open the door to restoration.

Leaders should also focus on creating a culture of accountability, where mistakes are used as learning opportunities rather than sources of blame. This approach encourages openness and helps to restore faith in leadership's intent and capability. Organisations that emphasise accountability, especially from the top down, are more likely to see a faster restoration of trust and engagement.

An example of rebuilding trust in practice is Toyota. After its large-scale recalls in the late 2000s, the company took full responsibility for the mistakes, apologised publicly, and committed to improving quality control. Through transparent communication and systematic changes, Toyota was able to regain its customer trust and restore its global reputation.

Trust and Organisational Culture

When embedded in the culture, trust becomes a sustainable advantage. Organisations where trust is part of the culture experience lower turnover, higher employee morale, and better resilience in times of crisis. Leaders who foster a trusting culture encourage their teams to take calculated risks, innovate, and collaborate without fear of blame or retribution.

Creating a culture of trust requires ongoing commitment. It is not enough to assume trust will develop organically. Trust must be an intentional part of leadership development programmes and be reinforced through regular team-building initiatives. Building trust through every layer of the organisation can empower employees to contribute their best, knowing that their leaders and peers have their back.

For example, at Netflix, the culture of trust is woven into every policy, including their famously flexible vacation policy. By trusting employees to manage their own time and act responsibly, Netflix creates an environment where trust leads to greater ownership and accountability across the board.

Conclusion: Trust Is a Continuous Journey

Building, maintaining, and rebuilding trust is a continuous process. Leaders must commit to being vigilant and intentional about how they foster trust within their organisations. This requires a deep understanding that trust is not static; it requires nurturing and can be influenced by numerous factors, including changing business environments, employee experiences, and organisational outcomes.

As a leader, it is essential to continually evaluate and adapt trust-building strategies, ensuring they resonate with the evolving needs of the workforce. This adaptability is crucial in today's dynamic world, where change is the only constant. Leaders who embrace a mindset of ongoing learning and openness will find that they can navigate challenges more effectively while strengthening trust within their teams.

Finally, trust must be viewed as a shared responsibility within the organisation. While leadership sets the tone, every employee plays a role in building and maintaining trust through their actions, interactions, and behaviours. Creating a high-trust environment requires collaboration and commitment from all levels of the organisation, transforming trust from a leadership initiative into a collective endeavour.

By making trust a fundamental pillar of organisational culture, leaders can unlock unprecedented levels of engagement, collaboration, and performance. As organisations navigate complex challenges and strive for success, the power of trust will be their greatest asset.

Reflection: Questions for Leaders

To build, maintain, and rebuild trust within your organisation, ask yourself:

- Are we fostering a culture of trust at all levels? Are we as leaders demonstrating consistent behaviour that aligns with our values and builds trust with employees?
- How do we handle breaches of trust? When trust is broken, are we acknowledging it, taking responsibility, and implementing changes to rebuild it?
- Are we creating a safe environment for accountability? Do our teams feel safe admitting mistakes and taking risks, knowing they won't face unnecessary blame?
- Is trust embedded in our leadership development? Are we training and developing leaders to model trust-building behaviours and to foster it within their teams?
- How transparent are our communications? Are we being open with employees about decisions and actions, especially during difficult times, to reinforce trust?

Chapter 6

Adaptability – Embracing Change for Continuous Growth

In today's fast-paced and ever-evolving business environment, adaptability is more than a desirable trait. It's a necessity. The ability to embrace change, adjust strategies, and continuously evolve is at the heart of long-term organisational success. Companies that fail to adapt risk stagnation or, worse, becoming obsolete in the face of disruption.

Adaptability is not just about reactive flexibility. It's about proactively preparing the organisation, its leaders, and its employees, to anticipate changes and respond effectively. This requires fostering a mindset where change is seen not as a threat but as an opportunity for growth and improvement. Leaders must not only navigate change themselves but also create a culture that embraces it as part of everyday business.

The Role of Leaders in Cultivating Adaptability

Leaders must set the tone for adaptability by embodying an openness to change. They need to demonstrate resilience, agility, and a growth mindset. Leadership at all levels plays a crucial role in showing that change is a natural part of progress and that it can be handled with confidence and optimism. By doing so, leaders can reduce fear of the unknown and encourage their teams to lean into change.

One example of a company that exemplifies adaptability is Amazon. Since its inception, Amazon has continually expanded its operations beyond its original focus on books, adapting to market demands and technological advancements. Whether moving into cloud computing with Amazon Web Services or revolutionising logistics with same-day delivery, Amazon's culture of constant innovation and flexibility has been key to its dominance.

Building a Culture that Embraces Change

Adaptability doesn't come naturally to all organisations. Many companies struggle with resistance to change, particularly when it disrupts established routines or requires new skills. To counteract this, it is essential for leaders to foster a culture where change is viewed positively. This begins with communication, explaining not just what is changing but why the change is necessary and how it benefits both the organisation and its employees.

Encouraging a learning culture is a powerful way to support adaptability. By investing in continuous development and upskilling, organisations can empower employees to view change as an opportunity to grow rather than as a threat to their stability. It's also important to create an environment where experimentation and innovation are valued. Employees need to feel that they have the freedom to try new approaches, even if some fail. This not only fosters adaptability but also fuels creativity and innovation.

Overcoming Resistance to Change

Resistance to change is natural; humans are wired for predictability and comfort. However, when organisational culture resists change, it creates significant barriers to growth. The key to overcoming this resistance is understanding the root causes, which often stem from fear of the unknown, lack of information, or a feeling of loss of control.

Leaders must address these concerns head-on. This involves transparent communication, providing clear direction, and making the benefits of change tangible. Employees are more likely to embrace change when they understand how it aligns with their personal goals or job security. Additionally, involving employees in the change process, asking for their input, addressing their concerns, and celebrating small wins along the way can help alleviate resistance and build buy-in.

The Strategic Advantage of Adaptability

Adaptability doesn't just make an organisation more responsive to change; it provides a competitive advantage. Organisations that can anticipate shifts in market conditions, customer preferences, or technological advancements, are better positioned to innovate and stay ahead of competitors. Adaptability can also improve customer relationships, as companies that are able to adjust quickly to client needs tend to build stronger, more loyal partnerships.

For instance, the COVID-19 pandemic forced businesses worldwide to rethink their operations. Companies that were able to quickly shift to remote work, embrace digital transformation, and find new ways to serve their customers, not only survived but thrived. Adaptability allowed organisations to maintain continuity and even discover new opportunities for growth during a crisis.

Adaptability and Long-Term Growth

Adaptability is key to ensuring long-term growth in an unpredictable world. It allows organisations to pivot when necessary and to stay resilient through periods of uncertainty. However, fostering adaptability requires a continuous focus on learning and improvement. Leaders need to ensure that their teams are equipped with the skills and mindsets necessary to embrace change as a pathway to growth.

For lasting success, adaptability must be embedded into the organisation's DNA. This means promoting a continuous feedback loop where change is reviewed, lessons are learned, and adjustments are made. Over time, this creates a self-sustaining culture of adaptability, where change is no longer seen as disruptive but as a constant and expected part of the organisation's evolution.

Developing Adaptability Through Mindset Shifts

A core element of adaptability lies in developing a mindset that is not only open to change but actively seeks it out. This involves cultivating a *growth mindset* –

a term popularised by psychologist Carol Dweck – which contrasts with a fixed mindset. Individuals and organisations with a fixed mindset tend to avoid challenges, view effort as fruitless, and feel threatened by the success of others. On the other hand, a growth mindset sees challenges as opportunities to learn, believes that effort leads to mastery, and celebrates the success of others as inspiration. Leaders who encourage this kind of thinking help their teams build resilience and adaptability.

To implement this, leaders need to create an environment where failure is viewed not as something to be feared but as a valuable learning opportunity. Google's famous mantra, 'fail fast, fail often', underlines the importance of learning from mistakes quickly and adapting strategies accordingly. In organisations where employees feel safe to take calculated risks without fear of blame, adaptability becomes a natural by-product of daily operations.

Empowering Teams to Make Decisions

One of the ways to build adaptability is by empowering teams to make decisions. In traditional hierarchical structures, decisions are often made by the top tier of leadership, which can create bottlenecks and slow the organisation's ability to respond to change. However, organisations that distribute decision-making power to lower levels can respond more quickly and dynamically to emerging challenges and opportunities.

For instance, Zappos – an online retailer known for its customer service – operates on a *holacracy* system, where employees are given the authority to make decisions within their roles. This decentralised approach allows the company to be highly responsive to customer needs and operational changes without having to go through layers of approval. Leaders in adaptable organisations focus on setting clear goals and frameworks, but they give teams the autonomy to execute plans as they see fit.

Agility in Organisational Structures

Adaptability also requires a review of the organisational structure itself. Traditional, rigid structures can be a hindrance to change, whereas more agile, flexible frameworks allow for faster decision-making and response times. An agile structure involves cross-functional teams that can quickly adapt to changes in market conditions or internal dynamics. By fostering collaboration across different departments, organisations can eliminate silos, improve communication, and be better equipped to handle changes as they arise.

Take the example of Spotify, which employs a *squad* system. These squads operate almost like mini start-ups within the company, each focusing on a specific aspect of Spotify's business, from user experience to backend infrastructure. The autonomy granted to these squads enables them to quickly innovate and adapt, ensuring that Spotify remains agile in an industry that is constantly evolving.

Continuous Feedback Loops and Adaptability

In the context of fostering adaptability, continuous feedback loops are critical. Organisations that rely on annual or infrequent feedback mechanisms often miss out on valuable insights that could drive timely changes. Instead, leaders need to implement systems that facilitate regular feedback at all levels of the organisation, allowing for real-time adjustments. This requires creating an open and transparent culture where feedback is both given and received constructively.

A good example of this is Netflix, where feedback is given frequently and openly as part of its 'culture of candour'. Employees are encouraged to give direct feedback, and leaders are expected to actively seek input from their teams. This ensures that any potential barriers to adaptability are identified early and addressed swiftly, enabling the company to remain responsive and competitive.

Balancing Stability with Adaptability

While adaptability is crucial, it must be balanced with a certain level of stability. Organisations need a strong foundation of core values, vision, and purpose that remains consistent, even as strategies and operations shift to adapt to change. Leaders must, therefore, strike a balance between maintaining the organisation's identity and mission, while being flexible enough to evolve in response to external pressures.

One of the key challenges for leaders is to avoid 'change fatigue', where continuous changes without clear direction or purpose lead to employee burnout. Leaders must ensure that their teams understand not only the need for change but how it aligns with the organisation's long-term goals. Providing context and reassurance during times of change can help mitigate the stress and uncertainty that often accompanies adaptability efforts.

Adapting to External Pressures

In today's volatile business environment, external pressures such as technological advancements, regulatory changes, or shifts in consumer preferences, can significantly impact organisational performance. Leaders who successfully embed adaptability into their company culture understand the need to monitor and respond to these external influences regularly. They build a culture of *proactive adaptation* rather than reactive scrambling.

One example of this is Kodak, a company that famously failed to adapt to the rise of digital photography, despite being one of the early inventors of the technology. Kodak's downfall was largely due to its unwillingness to shift away from its core product, film, which had historically driven its success. On the other hand, companies like Apple and Amazon have thrived precisely because they continually reinvent themselves in response to external pressures. Apple, once a computer company, is now a dominant player in smartphones, wearables, and entertainment. Amazon, initially an online bookstore, has grown into a global e-commerce and cloud computing giant by maintaining a culture of agility and innovation.

These examples highlight the necessity for organisations to embrace change not as a threat, but as a driver for continuous growth. By monitoring industry trends, staying close to customer needs, and being willing to pivot, companies can ensure their long-term survival and success.

Leadership's Role in Modelling Adaptability

Leadership plays a critical role in modelling adaptability. If leaders resist change, it sends a signal throughout the organisation that the status quo is acceptable, even when it becomes clear that the market or internal dynamics are shifting. Leaders must be willing to evolve their thinking, remain curious, and engage with new ideas, even if it means challenging their own previous strategies.

An effective way to do this is through *adaptive leadership* – a concept introduced by leadership expert Ronald Heifetz. Adaptive leadership focuses on the ability to lead through change, by encouraging organisations to experiment, take smart risks, and continuously learn from their environment. Rather than offering all the answers, adaptive leaders facilitate problem-solving by involving others in the process, fostering a culture where creativity and flexibility can flourish.

Moreover, leadership development programmes should integrate training on adaptability, ensuring that emerging leaders are prepared to guide their teams through future transformations. This investment in leadership agility strengthens the entire organisation's ability to pivot and grow, even in the face of uncertainty.

Creating a Culture of Continuous Learning

Another key factor in fostering adaptability is cultivating a culture of continuous learning. Organisations that invest in learning and development (L&D) programmes encourage their employees to constantly upgrade their skills and stay ahead of industry trends. This is particularly important in the current digital age, where technologies are evolving faster than ever before.

Many companies, including Microsoft, have adopted a 'learn-it-all' culture, as opposed to a 'know-it-all' culture. Microsoft CEO Satya Nadella, credited with revitalising the company, actively encourages employees to be curious, to learn new skills, and to be open to new ways of thinking. By embedding this learning mentality at all levels of the organisation, Microsoft has been able to continuously adapt and innovate.

Investing in employee development ensures that teams are equipped with the skills and knowledge needed to respond effectively to both internal and external changes. It also fosters an environment where employees feel empowered to suggest improvements, take ownership of their learning journeys, and contribute to the organisation's adaptability in meaningful ways.

Adaptability: The Lifeblood of Modern Organisations

In today's rapidly evolving business environment, the ability to adapt isn't just a beneficial trait – it's essential for survival. Organisations that cling rigidly to outdated processes, resist change, or overlook shifting market demands, often find themselves left behind. On the flip side, those that embrace adaptability develop a competitive edge, staying relevant and innovative in an increasingly complex and interconnected world.

Adaptability, at its core, is the ability to shift perspectives, adopt new approaches, and pivot when necessary, without losing sight of the organisation's overarching goals. It's a mindset as much as it is a skill, and it is critical for leaders to model this behaviour to foster a culture where change is seen as an opportunity rather than a threat.

In adaptive organisations, change is not feared. Instead, it's woven into the fabric of how things are done, from decision-making to daily operations. Leaders who promote adaptability encourage their teams to think flexibly, respond to challenges proactively, and view setbacks as learning opportunities.

Leading Adaptability: The Role of the Senior Leader

Leadership plays a pivotal role in embedding adaptability within an organisation. The most effective leaders are those who demonstrate an openness to change themselves, setting the tone for the rest of the organisation. Leaders must be able to navigate ambiguity, uncertainty, and even failure, while maintaining confidence in their long-term vision.

Self-awareness and emotional intelligence are key traits for adaptable leaders. Leaders who are in tune with their own emotional responses to change are better equipped to guide their teams through transitions. This involves showing resilience, flexibility, and empathy, particularly when navigating periods of significant disruption. For example, leaders who maintain calm and offer clear direction during times of uncertainty help reduce anxiety and boost morale within their teams.

Leaders need to ensure that adaptability is viewed not as a one-off reaction to external events but as a strategic pillar. This means embedding adaptability into the organisation's values and behaviours, ensuring it is part of every employee's mindset. A culture of adaptability is one that embraces continuous improvement and agility in the face of change.

Building a Culture of Learning and Agility

Adaptability is inextricably linked to a commitment to lifelong learning. In an adaptable organisation, there is an expectation that employees at all levels remain curious, continually develop new skills, and seek out new knowledge.

A culture of learning agility ensures that individuals are not just prepared for the next change but can also anticipate it. This includes encouraging cross-functional learning, where employees from different departments share insights and skills, which can lead to greater innovation. Leaders can support this by investing in learning and development initiatives, encouraging self-directed learning, and providing employees with opportunities to broaden their skill sets.

Agile methodologies, commonly associated with software development, can also be applied more broadly within organisations to support adaptability. Agile practices involve iterative processes, feedback loops, and a focus on quick pivots when necessary. By embedding these practices across different teams, organisations can enhance their ability to more effectively react to market shifts, customer demands, and technological advancements.

Overcoming Resistance to Change

While adaptability is highly valued, it is often met with resistance, especially in organisations that have enjoyed prolonged success with a particular approach. Change can trigger discomfort, fear, and anxiety, particularly if it is perceived as a threat to job security or established norms.

To address this, leaders must work to overcome this resistance by fostering a positive mindset towards change. This begins by communicating the benefits of change in a clear, relatable way. Instead of presenting change as an inevitable disruption, leaders can frame it as an exciting opportunity for growth, both for the organisation and the individual.

Building trust during transitions is crucial. Employees are more likely to embrace change when they trust their leaders and believe in the direction the organisation is heading. This means being transparent about why change is necessary, what the expected outcomes are, and how individuals will be supported throughout the process. When leaders engage in regular, two-way communication during times of change, it fosters an atmosphere of collaboration rather than resistance.

Nokia and Apple's Divergent Paths

A poignant example of how adaptability (or lack thereof) can shape an organisation's future is the story of Nokia and Apple. Once a dominant player in the mobile phone market, Nokia's reluctance to embrace change led to its decline. Despite clear signals that the market was shifting towards smartphones, Nokia clung to its existing product lines and failed to innovate quickly enough.

In contrast, Apple – under the leadership of Steve Jobs – embraced innovation and adaptability. By continuously pushing boundaries, introducing revolutionary products, and responding to customer demands with agility, Apple became a global leader in technology. The company's success was a direct result of its ability to adapt to change faster and more effectively than its competitors.

The Importance of Feedback Loops

Feedback loops are critical in ensuring an organisation remains adaptable. They allow for the collection and analysis of data, employee insights, and customer feedback, which can be used to inform decision-making. By integrating regular feedback mechanisms, leaders can stay attuned to emerging trends, challenges, and opportunities, making it easier to pivot when necessary.

Organisations that operate without effective feedback loops often fail to notice the early warning signs of change until it's too late. Whether it's shifts in customer preferences, technological advancements, or internal cultural shifts, the lack of a feedback loop can result in slow reactions and missed opportunities. Feedback should be encouraged at all levels, from senior leadership to frontline staff, ensuring that the organisation remains agile and responsive.

Conclusion: Adaptability as a Lifelong Commitment

Adaptability is not a one-time initiative but an ongoing commitment. The organisations that thrive in today's fast-changing world are those that embed adaptability into their culture, systems, and leadership. By fostering a growth mindset, empowering teams to make decisions, and creating a culture of continuous learning, leaders can ensure their organisations remain resilient in the face of change.

More than ever, the ability to adapt has become a critical determinant of success. Whether facing technological disruptions, shifting market demands, or internal changes, leaders must encourage flexibility, agility, and openness to new ideas. This not only ensures the long-term viability of the organisation but also creates a work environment where employees feel empowered to grow and contribute to the future of the business.

By embracing change and fostering a culture that thrives on adaptability, leaders can unlock the potential for continuous growth and ensure that their organisations remain agile, competitive, and ready for whatever the future may bring.

Reflection: Questions for Leaders

To build a culture of adaptability, ask yourself:

- How well do we anticipate change?
  Are we proactively scanning the environment for potential shifts in the market, technology, or customer preferences?
- Are we promoting a learning culture?
  Do we invest in the ongoing development of our employees to ensure they have the skills to adapt to new challenges?
- How do we respond to resistance?
  Are we addressing employee concerns and fears openly and constructively when change is introduced?

- Are we modelling adaptability as leaders?
  Do we as leaders demonstrate flexibility, openness to new ideas, and resilience in the face of challenges?
- How are we measuring adaptability?
  Do we track our organisation's ability to respond to changes and adjust strategies effectively, and are we learning from past experiences?

Chapter 7

Celebrate Success –
Reinforce the Positive

Celebrate Success: Reinforce the Positive

Recognising and celebrating achievements within an organisation is not just about patting people on the back; it's a fundamental part of embedding a positive culture. When done right, celebrating success acts as a powerful motivator, reinforcing the behaviours that align with the organisation's values and driving both individual and team performance. Success stories become cultural markers, setting the tone for what is valued and rewarded within the organisation.

Celebrating Success to Reinforce Values

Celebrations should align with the company's core values. When individuals or teams exhibit behaviours that reflect the organisation's values, recognising these efforts serves as a clear message to others about what the company stands for. It's not just about results; it's about how those results are achieved.

For example, if one of your core values is collaboration, don't just reward the person who achieves a result independently. Celebrate those who work well with others to deliver outcomes. If innovation is a core value, recognise the team that introduced a creative solution, even if it wasn't implemented immediately.

Leaders should be deliberate about this alignment between celebration and values. Every success story is an opportunity to demonstrate that the organisation truly lives by its principles. This encourages others to embody these same values in their work.

Making Celebrations Inclusive

For celebrations to have their maximum impact, they must be inclusive. This means going beyond recognising only the most visible achievements or the star performers. Every employee, at every level, should feel they have the opportunity to contribute to the success of the organisation and be recognised for doing so.

Celebrating small wins along the way is crucial, especially in larger organisations where individuals may feel that their contributions are easily overlooked. Creating platforms, whether it's regular shoutouts in team meetings, an internal newsletter, or an online recognition portal, helps ensure that everyone's efforts are visible.

Inclusivity in celebration also means taking into account diverse preferences for how people like to be recognised. Some may enjoy public recognition, while others may prefer a more private acknowledgment. Tailoring recognition to the individual can make the experience more meaningful and impactful.

The Role of Leaders in Celebrations

The most senior leaders play a pivotal role in setting the tone for how success is celebrated. When leaders take the time to acknowledge and celebrate success, it signals to everyone that such recognition is a priority. This behaviour should cascade down the hierarchy, creating a culture where managers at every level make it a point to celebrate the achievements of their teams.

Leaders who are visibly engaged in celebrating success build a stronger connection with their employees. It shows that they are aware of the efforts being made on the ground and are genuinely appreciative of them. This connection can significantly boost morale and strengthen the bond between leadership and staff.

It's also essential that leaders are consistent in their approach to celebration. Recognition should not be reserved only for the major, headline-grabbing achievements. Employees need to feel that success is celebrated regularly, and that recognition is fairly distributed, rather than concentrated on a few high-profile individuals.

Balancing Celebration with Continuous Improvement

While celebrating success is vital, it's also important to balance it with a culture of continuous improvement. Success should not breed complacency. Instead, it should be a springboard for further growth and development. Recognising achievements should be accompanied by reflection. What did we do well? What can we learn from this experience? How can we replicate this success in the future?

Celebrations should inspire people to aim higher, knowing that their efforts will be recognised and valued. By coupling celebration with reflection and a growth mindset, leaders can create a culture where success is a journey, not a destination.

Celebrating Milestones in Long-Term Projects

In organisations with long-term goals or projects, it's especially important to celebrate interim milestones. Waiting until the end of a multiyear project to celebrate can lead to burnout and a loss of momentum. By breaking projects into smaller, achievable goals and celebrating these along the way, organisations can maintain motivation and sustain high levels of engagement.

This approach also helps keep teams focused and aligned with the organisation's culture. Each milestone becomes an opportunity to reaffirm the values guiding the project and ensure that the team continues working in a way that reflects the broader cultural objectives.

Embedding Celebration into Daily Operations

Celebrating success doesn't have to be limited to grand gestures or formal events. In fact, the most effective celebrations are often those that are embedded into the day-to-day operations of the organisation. Simple, consistent recognition, whether through a 'thank you' email, a mention in a meeting, or a small token of appreciation, can go a long way in reinforcing positive behaviours.

Organisations can also create formal mechanisms for recognition, such as an employee of the month award or a peer-nominated system. These programmes should be easy to access and participate in, ensuring that recognition becomes part of the fabric of the organisation, rather than an occasional event.

Celebrating success is a vital aspect of reinforcing the desired organisational culture. When leaders actively acknowledge and celebrate achievements, they not only boost morale but also create an environment where positive behaviours are recognised and repeated. It is critical to recognise the importance of celebrating successes, the different ways to implement a recognition culture, and the long-term benefits of reinforcing positive outcomes within the organisation.

The Power of Recognition

Recognition can take many forms, from simple verbal praise to formal awards and recognition programmes. The key is to ensure that celebrations are aligned with the organisation's values and culture. Recognising individual and team achievements reinforces the behaviours and outcomes that contribute to the organisation's goals, encouraging others to aspire to similar successes.

Impact on Employee Engagement

Research consistently shows that employees who feel recognised for their contributions are more engaged and motivated. According to a study by Gallup, employees who receive regular recognition and praise are more productive, more engaged, and more likely to stay with their organisation. This underscores the idea that recognition is not just nice to have; it is a critical component of a healthy workplace culture.

Additionally, celebrating success can foster a sense of belonging and community within the workplace. When achievements are shared and celebrated, it creates a collective identity and reinforces the idea that everyone is working towards common goals.

Aligning Celebrations with Core Values

To make celebrations meaningful, it is essential to align them with the organisation's core values and behaviours. For instance, if one of the core values is collaboration, then team achievements should be highlighted in recognition events. This alignment helps to create a cohesive message about what success looks like within the organisation and encourages behaviours that are in line with the desired culture.

Leaders should consider establishing a recognition programme that is not only focused on individual achievements but also on team dynamics and collaborative efforts. This could involve peer-to-peer recognition platforms where employees can publicly acknowledge each other's contributions. Such systems can help to cultivate a culture where appreciation is woven into the fabric of everyday interactions.

Recognising the Power of Peer-to-Peer Recognition

One of the most powerful forms of recognition often comes not from leadership, but from peers. When employees acknowledge each other's efforts, it builds camaraderie and reinforces the idea that recognition isn't only the job of managers. Peer-to-peer recognition programmes encourage everyone to look for and acknowledge the good work happening around them, fostering a more cohesive and positive environment.

For instance, many organisations introduce 'kudos' systems, where employees can send public or private shoutouts to their colleagues for going above and beyond. These systems are particularly effective when they're tied to the organisation's values, enabling employees to recognise how their peers exemplify core principles like collaboration, innovation, or integrity. This kind of culture-building tool increases engagement and helps create a more collaborative and supportive workplace.

Celebrating Success Across Generations

With multiple generations working side by side, from Baby Boomers to Gen Z, it's important to recognise that different employees might value different types of recognition. While some may prefer formal, public acknowledgements like employee of the month awards, others might value a more personalised or private form of appreciation, such as a one-on-one conversation with a manager or a note of thanks.

Understanding these preferences is key to designing a celebration system that resonates with the entire workforce. Leaders and HR professionals need to ensure that they are flexible and open to customising the way they celebrate success to meet the diverse needs of their teams. For example, younger employees may appreciate digital recognition platforms that are easily shareable, while older employees might value more traditional, face-to-face recognition.

Creating a Legacy of Success

Celebration of success should not be seen as a onetime event or as something only to be done at the end of a project. Instead, the most successful organisations treat recognition as an ongoing practice. This means building a legacy of success stories that can be referenced and built upon in the future.

Highlighting past successes during onboarding or training sessions for new employees helps them to understand what kind of culture they are joining. These success stories become part of the organisation's narrative, creating a sense of continuity and a foundation for future achievements.

Additionally, establishing a tradition of celebrating success sends a clear message that the company values long-term contributions and recognises both individual and team efforts in shaping the organisation's history.

The Psychology of Celebrating Success

Celebrating success taps into a powerful psychological principle: positive reinforcement. When individuals or teams are recognised for their efforts and accomplishments, they are more likely to repeat the behaviours that led to those successes. This is rooted in behavioural psychology, where rewarding a desired behaviour increases the likelihood of it being repeated. For organisations, this means that celebrating successes, no matter how small or large, can build momentum towards continuous achievement and greater engagement.

Research has shown that when employees feel valued and recognised, their levels of motivation and job satisfaction increase. However, it's important for leaders to understand that success doesn't always have to be a monumental achievement. Regular acknowledgment of daily wins or incremental progress reinforces a culture of positivity and continuous improvement. This also aligns with Maslow's Hierarchy of Needs, where recognition contributes to individuals' sense of esteem, which in turn drives higher performance.

Embedding Celebration into Organisational Culture

Organisations that are intentional about celebrating success create a sense of shared achievement, which fosters team cohesion and strengthens relationships among colleagues. Celebrating success can take many forms, from formal recognition programmes to informal praise in team meetings. What's most important is that celebrations are authentic, timely, and meaningful.

Authenticity matters because employees can easily detect when praise feels forced or insincere. Leaders must focus on recognising genuine efforts and successes rather than feeling pressured to praise for the sake of it. Additionally, timeliness is key. Recognising success immediately after it happens makes the impact more significant. Waiting too long to celebrate might diminish the feeling of accomplishment and momentum.

Google's 'Peer Bonuses'

Google offers a unique approach to celebrating success through its peer bonus programme, which allows employees to nominate their colleagues for a small financial reward when they observe them going above and beyond in their roles. This system encourages a culture of recognition that's not just driven from the top down but also across peers. It makes celebration a collaborative effort, giving individuals at all levels the chance to acknowledge one another. This approach strengthens trust and mutual respect, contributing to a high-performance culture.

Creating Lasting Impact with Personalised Celebrations

While public recognition is effective, personalising how successes are celebrated adds another layer of impact. Leaders should be attuned to the different ways individuals prefer to be acknowledged. Some employees might appreciate public recognition, while others may prefer a private conversation or personal note of appreciation. Tailoring celebrations to the individual shows that leaders understand and respect the uniqueness of their team members.

For example, one employee might thrive on verbal praise in front of their peers, while another may value opportunities for professional development or additional responsibility as recognition for their hard work. This personalisation not only increases the impact of the celebration but also builds stronger relationships between leaders and employees.

Success Is More Than the End Goal: Celebrating Effort and Progress

In many organisations, there's a tendency to reserve celebrations for when big goals are met, project completions, hitting sales targets, or winning new business. While these milestones certainly deserve celebration, there's also immense value in recognising the effort that leads up to these outcomes.

Celebrating progress helps maintain momentum, especially for long-term projects where the end goal might feel distant. It also keeps employees engaged and motivated throughout the process. Regularly acknowledging milestones along the way fosters a culture of perseverance and resilience, where employees feel appreciated for their ongoing contributions rather than waiting for the final payoff.

This ties into the concept of intrinsic motivation, recognising the satisfaction of progress and the learning that happens throughout the journey, not just the outcome. When leaders highlight progress and effort, they create a space where employees feel more comfortable taking risks and innovating, knowing their hard work won't go unnoticed, even if the end result isn't immediately realised.

Reinforcing Positivity Through Team Celebrations

Celebrating success isn't just about individual recognition; it's also a powerful tool for building and maintaining team cohesion. By highlighting team achievements, leaders can reinforce the importance of collaboration and collective effort.

Team celebrations can range from formal events, like team lunches, recognition ceremonies, or team building activities, to more informal gestures, such as shout-outs in meetings or shared acknowledgments in group chats. These moments serve to reinforce the idea that everyone's contributions matter and that success is often a shared outcome.

Moreover, team celebrations can break down silos and encourage cross-functional collaboration. When employees from different departments or teams are brought together to celebrate joint successes, it fosters a greater sense of unity and shared purpose across the organisation.

The Ripple Effect: How Celebrating Success Impacts Organisational Culture

Celebrating success doesn't just motivate the individuals or teams being recognised; it has a ripple effect that influences the entire organisation. When employees see their peers being acknowledged, it reinforces the behaviours that are valued within the organisation. It sets a standard for what success looks like and how it will be rewarded.

Frequent celebrations contribute to a positive work environment, which boosts overall morale. Organisations with a culture of recognition tend to experience lower turnover rates and higher levels of employee engagement. This is because employees are more likely to stay in environments where they feel their efforts are appreciated, and where they believe they are contributing to something larger than themselves.

In contrast, organisations that fail to celebrate success risk creating a culture of complacency or even resentment. When employees feel that their hard work goes unnoticed, they may become disengaged or disillusioned. Over time, this can lead to lower productivity, increased turnover, and a toxic work culture where employees are only focused on meeting the bare minimum.

The Impact of Celebrating Success

Psychologically, recognising success can have a profound impact on employees' mental health and motivation. Studies in positive psychology show that frequent and meaningful recognition helps to reinforce self-esteem, a sense of belonging, and job satisfaction. Employees who feel valued and recognised are far more likely to remain engaged in their roles and contribute fully to their teams.

Celebrations also trigger the release of dopamine, the 'feel-good' neurotransmitter, which reinforces a cycle of motivation and achievement. When employees are regularly recognised, they are more likely to seek out opportunities to continue performing at their best. This creates a positive feedback loop where success leads to further success.

Celebrating Failure as Part of Success

Though it may seem counterintuitive, an important aspect of celebrating success is recognising the role of failure in the journey. In an innovative and forward-thinking culture, failures are not something to be hidden or ignored. Instead, they are valuable learning opportunities that can pave the way for future successes.

Encouraging employees to take risks and celebrate lessons learned from their failures promotes a growth mindset within the organisation. When teams feel safe to take calculated risks, knowing they won't be punished for honest mistakes, they are more likely to innovate and push the organisation forward. This openness to learning, coupled with celebrations of resilience, reinforces a culture where success is defined not just by outcomes, but by the courage to take bold actions.

Diverse Ways to Celebrate Success

Celebrating success does not have to be limited to formal events. It can be integrated into daily routines and team meetings. Here are several strategies to effectively celebrate success:

1. **Public Recognition:** Use team meetings, newsletters, or internal communications to publicly acknowledge individual and team accomplishments. This not only highlights successes but also encourages others to strive for recognition.
2. **Incentive Programmes:** Implement reward systems where employees earn points or accolades for demonstrating desired behaviours or achieving specific goals. These can be exchanged for tangible rewards such as gift cards, extra time off, or experiences.
3. **Celebratory Events:** Host regular events, such as team lunches or after-work gatherings, to celebrate milestones. These informal settings can strengthen relationships and foster a sense of camaraderie among employees.
4. **Highlighting Stories:** Create a platform for employees to share success stories and the journeys behind them. This not only highlights

achievements but also provides inspiration and learning opportunities for others.

5. **Personalised Recognition:** Tailor recognition to individual preferences. Some employees may prefer public acknowledgment, while others may appreciate a private note of thanks. Understanding these preferences can make recognition more meaningful.

Long-term Benefits of Celebrating Success

The long-term benefits of fostering a culture of celebration and recognition are profound. When employees feel valued and appreciated, they are more likely to exhibit higher levels of job satisfaction, increased productivity, and a greater commitment to the organisation's goals.

An organisation that celebrates its successes is more resilient in the face of challenges. By focusing on positive outcomes, employees are reminded of their collective capabilities and the strengths of their team. This mindset can help to reduce stress and improve overall workplace morale.

Conclusion: Cultivating a Recognition Culture

In conclusion, celebrating success is not merely an optional aspect of organisational culture; it is a crucial strategy for reinforcing positive behaviours and outcomes. By actively recognising achievements, organisations can enhance employee engagement, foster a sense of belonging, and promote a culture that aligns with their core values.

As leaders commit to building a recognition culture, they pave the way for continuous improvement and sustained success. This emphasis on celebrating wins, no matter how small, ensures that the organisation remains focused on positive growth and is well-equipped to navigate future challenges.

Reflection: Questions for Leaders

To foster a culture of recognition and celebration within your organisation, consider the following questions:

- How frequently are we recognising individual and team successes?
- Are our recognition efforts aligned with our core values and desired behaviours?
- What systems do we have in place to ensure that recognition is meaningful and inclusive?
- How can we make celebrations a regular part of our organisational culture?
- Are we encouraging peer-to-peer recognition, and how can we strengthen this practice?

Chapter 8

Tough Conversations –
When Culture Demands Change

Building and maintaining an organisational culture that aligns with core values and ensuing behaviours is an ongoing process, and there will inevitably be moments when difficult decisions must be made. When certain individuals resist the desired culture, or when behaviours don't align with the agreed upon values, leaders must be prepared to address these issues head-on. While it's often possible to coach and develop employees to adapt to the culture, there are times when the hard truth is that some people simply won't change. In these cases, the uncomfortable reality may be that if you can't change the people, you may have to change the people.

This chapter explores how leaders can approach these tough situations and make decisions that preserve the integrity of the organisational culture, even when it involves difficult conversations or personnel changes.

Identifying the Cultural Misalignment

The first step in addressing cultural issues is identifying when and where misalignment occurs. Often, this can manifest in various ways:

1. **Behavioural Misalignment:** Individuals whose actions consistently contradict the organisation's values, such as demonstrating a lack of respect, accountability, or integrity.
2. **Resistance to Change:** Employees who refuse to adapt to new cultural expectations or resist initiatives aimed at embedding the desired culture.
3. **Toxic Influence:** Sometimes, it's not just about resistance but about individuals who actively undermine the culture, spreading negativity or engaging in destructive behaviours that affect the broader team.

Leaders need to be attuned to these signs and take swift action before misaligned behaviours become ingrained in the organisational fabric.

The Importance of Early Intervention

One of the most critical lessons for leaders when dealing with cultural misalignment is the importance of early intervention. Issues that go unaddressed often grow, not only causing deeper cultural fractures but also signalling to other employees that the organisation isn't serious about its values. Delayed action can erode trust in leadership and create a permissive environment where toxic behaviours become tolerated or normalised.

Open and Honest Conversations

The most effective way to begin tackling cultural misalignment is through candid, honest conversations. These conversations, while often uncomfortable, are crucial in providing clarity around expectations and allowing the individual an opportunity to course-correct.

When initiating these discussions, consider the following:

1. **Focus on the Values, Not the Person**: Frame the conversation around how their behaviour misaligns with the organisation's core values rather than attacking their character. This makes the conversation feel less personal and more about their fit with the culture.
2. **Be Clear and Direct**: Ambiguity can lead to misunderstanding. Be specific about which behaviours need to change and why they're misaligned with the culture.
3. **Provide Support**: Sometimes, individuals may struggle with change, not because of unwillingness but because they don't know how. Offer coaching or mentoring to help them adjust.
4. **Set Clear Expectations**: Outline what changes need to happen and by when, making it clear that failure to meet these expectations will result in further consequences.

Deciding When It's Time for Change

Despite best efforts, some individuals may not change, and their continued presence may undermine the culture the organisation is striving to build. As difficult as it may be, leaders must sometimes face the reality that if certain people don't align with the culture, it may be time for them to move on.

Making the Tough Call

The decision to let someone go due to cultural misalignment should never be taken lightly. It's essential to ensure that all avenues of coaching and support have been explored first. However, if the individual continues to exhibit behaviours that contradict the organisation's values, the leader must prioritise the broader health of the team and the organisation.

Here's how leaders can navigate this decision:

1. **Evaluate the Impact**: Assess how the individual's behaviour is impacting the team and the culture. Are they demoralising others or causing friction? If their behaviour is toxic, the cost of keeping them may outweigh the potential benefits of retaining them.
2. **Consider the Message**: Failing to act sends a message to the rest of the organisation that cultural misalignment is tolerated. Removing someone who is not living up to the values reinforces the organisation's commitment to its culture.
3. **Transparency in the Process**: Be as transparent as possible (while maintaining confidentiality) about why certain decisions are made. This reinforces the importance of values-based leadership and builds trust.

Navigating Organisational Resistance

It's important to acknowledge that making cultural changes, or enforcing cultural standards, can sometimes provoke resistance, not just from the individual but from within the broader organisation. Employees might push back, questioning why someone was let go, especially if that person was a high performer or held influence.

Leaders need to manage this resistance carefully. Transparent communication is key here. When employees understand that decisions are made in the best interest of preserving the culture, they are more likely to support those decisions. Furthermore, by clearly reinforcing the connection between behaviours and values, leaders can alleviate concerns about fairness and ensure that employees understand that high performance alone is not enough, cultural alignment is equally important.

Addressing Resistance Head-On

No matter how clear and compelling a culture may be, there will always be individuals or pockets of resistance within an organisation. Resistance to cultural change is natural, whether it stems from discomfort with new behaviours, fear of losing influence, or simply attachment to old ways of doing things. However, avoiding or downplaying these tensions can undermine progress and erode morale.

Senior leaders need to proactively address resistance by first understanding its root causes. This means engaging with employees at all levels of the organisation to uncover any underlying fears, concerns, or objections. In many cases, resistance isn't about the values themselves, but rather a fear of the unknown or uncertainty about how the changes will impact day-to-day work. By creating open channels for honest dialogue, leaders can alleviate some of these concerns and make adjustments to the rollout process if necessary.

Performance Management and Accountability

The process of shaping and reinforcing organisational culture requires leaders to hold people accountable for living out the chosen values. While leaders often celebrate successes and reward behaviours aligned with the company's culture, they must also address behaviours that contradict or undermine those values. Failure to confront these issues early on can create confusion among employees and weaken the credibility of the leadership team.

Performance management systems need to be closely aligned with the desired culture, including mechanisms for identifying and correcting behaviours that go against the grain. Clear expectations and feedback loops should be in place so that employees understand how their actions align with or diverge from the organisation's values. In some cases, this might mean difficult conversations, formal performance improvement plans, or even letting go of individuals who consistently refuse to embody the organisation's culture.

For example, in an organisation that prioritises transparency as a core value, leaders cannot tolerate information hoarding or a lack of openness in communication. If such behaviours are left unaddressed, employees will quickly realise that the organisation's stated values are nothing more than words, eroding trust in leadership and the overall culture.

Cultural Drift and the Role of Leadership

One of the greatest challenges in maintaining a strong organisational culture is preventing cultural drift, which occurs when there is a slow and subtle departure from the organisation's core values over time. This drift can happen when leaders become complacent, stop reinforcing the values, or allow minor deviations to go unchecked. While these small shifts may seem insignificant in isolation, they can accumulate and lead to a significant misalignment between the desired culture and the reality on the ground.

Leaders must be vigilant in recognising the early signs of cultural drift and take corrective action to bring the organisation back in line with its core values. This could involve re-engaging teams in discussions about the organisation's values, refreshing the communication strategy, or conducting periodic culture audits to assess how closely the organisation's behaviours align with the intended culture.

Handling Toxicity

Toxic behaviour is one of the most corrosive elements in an organisational culture. Whether it takes the form of gossip, bullying, backstabbing, or power struggles, toxicity can quickly spread and derail efforts to create a positive, supportive environment. The challenge for leaders is that toxicity often takes root subtly, manifesting in micro behaviours that are difficult to detect and easy to dismiss.

Leaders must take a zero-tolerance approach to toxic behaviours, even when they involve high performers or influential individuals. If toxic behaviour is left unchallenged, it sends a clear message to the rest of the organisation that results matter more than values.

This can lead to a dangerous split in the culture, where some employees feel protected from accountability based on their status or performance, while others feel disempowered and disengaged.

To combat toxicity, leaders should ensure that the organisation has clear policies in place for reporting and addressing inappropriate behaviour. Employees need to feel safe and supported when raising concerns, knowing that their complaints will be taken seriously and dealt with swiftly. By prioritising the emotional wellbeing of employees, leaders can create a culture that fosters trust, collaboration, and respect.

Cultural Champions and Difficult Conversations

Leaders can't tackle difficult cultural issues alone; they need support from cultural champions throughout the organisation. Cultural champions are employees who not only exemplify the organisation's values but also have the courage to call out misalignments when they see them. These individuals play a crucial role in identifying problems at the ground level and encouraging their peers to hold themselves and others accountable.

Cultural champions can be especially valuable when it comes to having difficult conversations. Not every leader will have direct access to the day-to-day interactions of employees, so having a network of individuals who can raise red flags and initiate constructive discussions is essential. These champions can bridge the gap between senior leadership and the broader workforce, helping to resolve issues before they escalate.

The Role of Emotional Intelligence in Managing Difficult Issues

One of the most valuable traits for leaders when addressing cultural challenges is emotional intelligence (EI). Leaders with high emotional intelligence are better equipped to navigate the delicate nature of difficult conversations, maintain empathy, and resolve conflicts without escalating tensions. When confronting individuals who are resistant to the desired culture, leaders must balance assertiveness with understanding, ensuring that employees feel heard and respected, even when corrective action is necessary.

Developing EI within the leadership team and encouraging it across the organisation can significantly improve the culture. This is particularly true when it comes to recognising the emotional drivers behind behaviours that clash with the company's values. By understanding why an employee is disengaged, for example, or why certain teams are resistant to change, leaders can more effectively address the root causes rather than just the symptoms.

Training in emotional intelligence should be a core component of leadership development programmes, helping leaders to not only model the organisation's values but also create an emotionally safe environment where difficult conversations can take place constructively.

Conflict Resolution as a Cultural Necessity

Conflict in any organisation is inevitable, but how it's handled can either strengthen or weaken the culture.

Leaders must ensure that conflict resolution aligns with the organisation's values, using it as an opportunity to reinforce the culture rather than allowing unresolved tensions to fester. For example, in a culture that values transparency, conflict should be dealt with openly and honestly, allowing all parties to express their viewpoints while working towards a solution that upholds the organisation's values.

Conflict should not be seen as a negative force but rather as an opportunity for growth. When managed effectively, it can lead to greater understanding, stronger relationships, and more innovative problem-solving. Leaders should model healthy conflict resolution and encourage it throughout the organisation, helping to create a culture where differences are seen as a source of strength rather than division.

Creating Safe Spaces for Cultural Feedback

A key element in sustaining a healthy organisational culture is creating safe spaces where employees can provide feedback without fear of retribution. These safe spaces can take many forms, whether through anonymous surveys, open forums, or one-on-one discussions, and should be designed to encourage honest, constructive input on how well the organisation is living up to its cultural ideals.

Without these feedback loops, leaders risk being unaware of cultural issues that are brewing beneath the surface. Employees may feel disengaged or disempowered if they perceive that their concerns are being ignored, or worse, punished. Establishing mechanisms for gathering feedback and acting on it demonstrates to employees that the leadership is genuinely committed to maintaining the culture and values of the organisation.

Furthermore, feedback shouldn't just come from top-down channels. Leaders should regularly seek input from employees at all levels of the organisation to ensure that the desired culture is being felt and embraced throughout. This open dialogue allows leaders to course-correct when necessary and make adjustments that keep the culture strong and adaptable to changing circumstances.

Turning Cultural Misfits into Opportunities for Growth

Rather than viewing cultural misalignment as solely a problem to be dealt with, leaders should approach it as an opportunity for growth, both for the individuals involved and for the organisation as a whole. Sometimes, cultural misfits can provide valuable perspectives that challenge the status quo in ways that lead to innovation and improved processes.

When an individual's behaviour conflicts with the organisation's values, leaders should engage them in a conversation that seeks to understand their perspective. There may be legitimate concerns that the current cultural direction is not working for certain parts of the business. By engaging in these conversations, leaders can find ways to refine and strengthen the culture, while giving employees a chance to grow and adapt.

Of course, if the cultural misalignment is too great and cannot be reconciled, leaders must have the courage to make difficult decisions regarding whether that individual can remain part of the organisation. However, where possible, these situations should be viewed as opportunities for positive change rather than punitive measures.

Navigating Resistance: The Inescapable Challenge

Change, especially when it involves altering the very fabric of an organisation's culture, often encounters resistance. This is natural. People are creatures of habit, and when long-standing behaviours, attitudes, and values are challenged, it can provoke fear, uncertainty, or defensiveness. As a leader, it's essential to anticipate this resistance and develop strategies to guide the organisation through it.

Resistance isn't always blatant. It can manifest in more subtle forms, such as passive compliance, superficial engagement, or behind-the-scenes dissent. Addressing resistance early is key, and that often means having tough, honest conversations with those who might be holding back cultural progress. These conversations must be approached with sensitivity but also with firm conviction, as leaving cultural misalignment unaddressed can derail the organisation's broader goals.

The most challenging aspect of navigating resistance is overcoming the emotional ties people have to the way things have always been done. Employees may feel that certain behaviours, even if inconsistent with the desired culture, are ingrained in the organisation's identity. Leaders must walk the line between respecting the past and leading the organisation toward a new, healthier future.

The Role of Transparency in Tough Conversations

One of the most critical elements in navigating difficult conversations about culture is transparency. Employees need to understand *why* a cultural shift is necessary, how it will benefit the organisation, and what role they play in making it happen. Leaders must be clear about the vision for the organisation's future and how the current culture, if misaligned, might be holding back progress.

Transparency should also extend to performance expectations. When having difficult conversations, leaders need to clearly outline what specific behaviours need to change, why they are not aligning with the organisation's values, and what steps must be taken to bring those behaviours into alignment. These conversations should focus on behaviours, not personalities, to prevent defensiveness and promote constructive dialogue.

Additionally, framing cultural change as an opportunity for growth, both personal and organisational, can help soften resistance. Employees should see cultural alignment as part of their development; a chance to be part of something greater and more cohesive.

Balancing Accountability with Empathy

Tough conversations about cultural misalignment must balance accountability with empathy. On the one hand, leaders must be firm in communicating that certain behaviours cannot continue. On the other hand, they need to be empathetic to the challenges employees face in adapting to new ways of working.

This balance is especially important when considering long-term, valued employees who might struggle to adapt to cultural changes. Rather than dismissing their challenges, leaders should seek to understand the root of their resistance. Is it a fear of losing relevance in the new culture? Is it a lack of confidence in their ability to adapt? Understanding these concerns opens the door to more compassionate, yet constructive conversations.

At the same time, leaders need to communicate that cultural misalignment cannot be tolerated indefinitely. If employees are unable or unwilling to embrace the new culture, tough decisions may have to be made. This might mean providing additional support and training, but in some cases, it may require making the hard choice to part ways with those who can't or won't adapt.

Identifying and Addressing Cultural Saboteurs

Not all resistance to cultural change is passive or unintentional. In some cases, there may be individuals within the organisation who actively work against the desired cultural shift. These cultural saboteurs can undermine progress, spread negativity, and even cause divisions among teams. Leaders must be vigilant in identifying these individuals and swiftly addressing their behaviour.

When dealing with cultural saboteurs, it's essential to confront the issue head-on. Ignoring the problem or hoping it will resolve itself can lead to a toxic undercurrent that poisons the organisation from within. Once identified, these individuals should be engaged in direct, honest conversations where leaders make it clear that their behaviour is not aligned with the organisation's values and will not be tolerated.

This doesn't mean every cultural saboteur needs to be dismissed immediately. Often, these individuals are influential, long-standing members of the organisation who might have valid concerns about the cultural shift. The key is to listen to their concerns but also set clear boundaries and expectations for their behaviour. In some cases, saboteurs may come around once they feel heard and understand the rationale for the change. However, if they continue to resist or sabotage the culture, leaders must be prepared to act decisively.

Holding Leaders Accountable for Cultural Alignment

It's crucial to remember that cultural change starts at the top. Senior leaders must model the behaviours they expect from the rest of the organisation, and this includes holding themselves accountable to the same standards. If leaders are seen as exempt from cultural expectations, it undermines the entire process and sends the message that the cultural change is not truly important.

Leaders should regularly seek feedback from their peers, direct reports, and even outside advisors to ensure they are practising what they preach. This could involve regular self-assessments, 360-degree feedback tools, or simply engaging in candid conversations with their teams. Leaders must be willing to adjust their behaviour if it is out of sync with the organisation's cultural goals.

One of the toughest conversations a leader can have is with themselves, confronting areas where they may be failing to live up to the values they want to instil in the organisation. Humility is a crucial trait for leaders in times of cultural change, as it allows them to acknowledge their own imperfections and model a commitment to continuous improvement.

The Consequences of Inaction: Why Tough Conversations Cannot Be Avoided

The cost of avoiding tough conversations about culture is high. When cultural misalignment is ignored or tolerated, it can lead to a deterioration of trust within the organisation. Employees who are committed to the culture will become frustrated and disengaged if they see others not being held accountable for failing to live up to the organisation's values.

In the long run, this can lead to attrition, especially among high performers who are invested in the culture. These individuals may seek out environments where the culture they value is consistently upheld. Additionally, failing to address cultural issues can cause a slow erosion of morale and productivity, as misaligned behaviours spread and become accepted norms.

To avoid these consequences, leaders must embrace the discomfort of tough conversations and view them as essential to the organisation's health and success. Cultural alignment is not a one-time event but an ongoing process that requires vigilance, courage, and the willingness to confront issues as they arise.

Conclusion: Culture Over Comfort

In conclusion, tackling cultural misalignment often requires difficult conversations and, at times, tough decisions. Leaders must be prepared to act in the best interest of the organisation's long-term culture, even when it means letting go of individuals who can't, or won't, align with the core values.

While these conversations and decisions are challenging, they are essential to maintaining the integrity of the culture. Leaders who prioritise culture over comfort demonstrate their commitment to creating an environment where values are upheld and employees are empowered to thrive.

Ultimately, by addressing cultural issues head-on, leaders can protect the health of their organisation and ensure that the culture remains a positive force that drives long-term success.

Reflection: Questions for Leaders

To help you navigate the complexities of addressing cultural misalignment, consider these questions:

- How proactive are we in identifying cultural misalignment within the organisation?
- Are we having honest and open conversations with employees whose behaviour contradicts our core values?
- Have we provided enough support and clear expectations for change?
- How do we ensure that our decisions regarding cultural fit are transparent and fair?
- Are we willing to make tough decisions to protect the culture, even if it means parting ways with high performers?

Chapter 9

Culture Permeation –
Measure and Master

Creating a thriving organisational culture is one thing but knowing whether it truly permeates throughout every level of the organisation is another. Leaders often set the tone from the top, believing their message will naturally cascade down. But without intentional measurement, it's hard to know whether the culture they envision actually exists in practice.

Measuring Culture: The Industry Standard

There are many reliable and well-established culture measurement instruments available today, both profiling and typing instrument types. These tools help organisations gain insights into the prevailing cultural dynamics, whether it's about understanding the type of culture (such as hierarchical, market-driven, or clan-oriented) or profiling how employees perceive and interact within that culture. Both profiling and typing Culture Measurement Surveys provide valuable data on employee engagement, workplace values, and perceived behaviours. These tools serve as useful diagnostics, giving leaders a big picture understanding of where the organisation stands in terms of culture.

However, while these instruments are helpful for profiling and typing, they often measure culture at an aggregate level. This approach risks diluting specific insights about how culture permeates across different levels of the organisation. Another challenge with aggregate measurements is that while they give you an overview, they can often overwhelm you with so much information that pinpointing the root cause of cultural blockages becomes difficult. And when it's hard to see where the issues lie, it's equally hard to fix them.

The Employee Survey Dilemma: More Harm Than Good?

Employee surveys are a common tool used by organisations to gather feedback on a variety of topics, including culture, engagement, and employee satisfaction. However, despite their widespread use, these surveys often fall into the trap of being little more than box-ticking exercises. This occurs when surveys are conducted without a genuine commitment to act on the results, leading to a growing disillusionment among employees.

When employees are asked for feedback and then see little or no meaningful change, it can damage trust between the workforce and leadership. In fact, failing to act on survey results can make the situation worse than if no survey had been conducted at all. Employees invest time and emotional energy in providing feedback, and when that input is ignored, it signals to them that their voices don't matter, reinforcing the very disengagement that the survey was intended to address.

It's not uncommon to hear employees express frustration after multiple rounds of surveys: '*Why do they keep asking us the same questions when nothing changes?'* This sentiment reveals the irony of many feedback initiatives. While they are often conducted with good intentions, the lack of follow-through results in deteriorating morale and a widening gap between leadership and employees.

The Box-Ticking Trap: The Dangers of Going Through the Motions

There's a significant risk in treating employee surveys as a mechanical process, disconnected from real cultural change. Companies may carry out surveys because they believe it's expected or required to demonstrate a commitment to employee engagement. However, if the process ends there, if the results are not analysed thoroughly, action plans are not developed, and communication back to employees is non-existent, it breeds cynicism.

The negative impact can ripple through the organisation, as employees stop seeing the point in participating in future surveys or initiatives. Over time, this lack of responsiveness chips away at trust and creates a culture of apathy, where even the most motivated employees become disillusioned. In such environments, the credibility of leadership suffers, and the organisation becomes mired in stagnation rather than growth.

To avoid this outcome, it's critical to treat employee surveys as living tools that feed directly into the decision-making process. This requires leadership to invest time, effort, and resources into closing the feedback loop, turning insights into actionable steps and communicating progress transparently.

The Power of Actionable Feedback Loops

One of the most critical aspects of using employee surveys effectively is having a clear strategy for what happens after the survey is completed. This means creating a well-defined process for analysing the data, understanding the key themes, and, most importantly, prioritising actions based on the feedback received.

Surveys should not be seen as an end in themselves but rather as the beginning of a feedback loop that helps refine and improve the organisation's culture. Leaders need to take the time to acknowledge the results and, where necessary, take corrective action to address any issues raised. Even when immediate change isn't possible, keeping the workforce informed about the status of these actions is essential for maintaining trust.

Clear, consistent communication is a vital part of this feedback loop. After the survey results are collected and analysed, leaders should openly share the findings with the entire organisation. This not only reinforces transparency but also demonstrates a commitment to continuous improvement. Employees need to know that their feedback has been heard, taken seriously, and is driving real change. Following up on the survey results and detailing what actions will be taken, or why certain changes aren't feasible, closes the loop and strengthens the connection between leadership and employees.

Employee Engagement and Performance: The Business Case for Culture Measurement

The connection between employee engagement and organisational performance has been well documented.

Studies consistently show that higher levels of employee engagement lead to improved productivity, better retention rates, and greater innovation within organisations. For example, according to research by Gallup, companies with high employee engagement levels are 21% more profitable and 17% more productive than those with low engagement.

When it comes to measuring culture permeation, this engagement performance link is crucial. A strong, aligned culture where values and behaviours are consistently lived out at all levels of the organisation creates an environment where employees feel empowered, valued, and motivated. This, in turn, drives better business outcomes.

However, achieving this level of engagement requires more than just conducting annual surveys. It requires ongoing attention to culture permeation, ensuring that the desired culture is not just a top-down mandate, but something that flows through every level of the organisation, influencing day-to-day behaviours and decisions.

The 360 Culture Permeation Survey (360 CPS) methodology developed during my PhD research is designed with this in mind. By assessing culture level by level, starting with the senior leadership team and moving downwards, the 360 CPS ensures that each layer of the organisation is aligned with the desired culture. This granular approach allows for pinpointing specific areas where cultural blockages might occur, making it easier to take targeted corrective actions.

Tailoring Surveys to Culture: A Bespoke Approach

Another common pitfall with generic employee surveys is that they fail to reflect the specific cultural values of the organisation. Off-the-shelf survey tools often assess broad areas like job satisfaction, engagement, or work-life balance, but they don't dig into the unique cultural dynamics that make one organisation different from another.

This is why I believe that customised survey questions tailored to the organisation's specific values and expected behaviours are so much more effective. The 360 CPS methodology is built around this principle. Rather than using generic questions, the survey is designed to measure how well the organisation's values and resulting behaviours are being lived at every level. This ensures that the feedback collected is directly tied to the cultural goals of the organisation, making the results much more actionable and relevant.

Tailoring the survey also sends a clear message to employees that the organisation is genuinely interested in aligning their behaviours with the stated values and not just conducting a superficial check on engagement. It reinforces the idea that culture isn't just a buzzword, but a critical part of how the business operates and thrives.

Avoiding the 'Once and Done' Mentality

Finally, one of the most damaging mistakes organisations make is assuming that a single culture survey or employee feedback session will solve all cultural issues. Culture measurement needs to be ongoing. Organisations are dynamic, constantly evolving entities, and so is their culture. Continuous measurement, rather than periodic check-ins, allows leaders to track progress over time and ensure that the culture remains aligned with the organisation's changing goals and environment.

By embedding culture measurement into the fabric of the organisation's processes, it becomes part of the organisation's DNA – a continuous process of improvement rather than a one-off event. This ensures that culture permeation is always a priority and that leaders are consistently aware of where they stand in relation to their cultural aspirations. Through my PhD research, I sought to address this very issue: How do we accurately measure whether a desired culture truly permeates every level of the organisation? From this research, I developed the 360 Culture Permeation Survey (360 CPS), a methodology specifically designed to measure cultural values and behaviours at each organisational level rather than aggregating all the data into one large pool.

This survey provides a more nuanced and focused measurement of cultural permeation, giving leaders a clearer sense of whether the values and behaviours they expect are being lived out across different departments, teams, and leadership levels. What sets the 360 CPS apart from other tools is that it's not just a general measurement of culture. It is specifically tailored to measure how well the chosen values and expected behaviours in an organisation are being demonstrated through observable behavioural measurement at each level.

Why Measure Level by Level?

When we measure culture at the aggregate level, the sheer amount of data can often obscure where cultural misalignments or blockages exist. Think of it like a river system: if you only look at the health of the entire river, you might miss the fact that a dam or blockage exists upstream, affecting everything downstream. By breaking down the measurements level by level, starting with the senior leadership team, we can pinpoint exactly where cultural blockages are happening and address them at the source.

By using the 360 CPS methodology, you start by assessing the behaviours of the senior leaders and their alignment with the chosen values of the organisation. These behaviours are critical because, as discussed in earlier chapters, the senior leadership team sets the example for the rest of the organisation. Once this level is assessed, you can work your way down the hierarchy, assessing the behaviours of middle management, team leaders, and frontline employees. This granular approach yields much richer information and is far more cost effective, because it allows you to focus interventions where they are needed most.

Tailored Questions for Tailored Culture

Another key difference between the 360 CPS and other instruments is that it is fully customisable. Most culture measurement tools are generic, providing a one-size-fits-all approach. But culture is never generic; it's unique to each organisation, shaped by its values, mission, and strategic goals. Therefore, the 360 CPS does not rely on preset questions. Instead, it tailors its survey questions to the specific values and behaviours chosen by the senior leadership of the organisation.

For example, if integrity is a core value, the 360 CPS will not just ask if employees believe the organisation values integrity. It will probe deeper, asking specific behavioural questions: *Do you see your leaders consistently make ethical decisions, even when under pressure? How often do team leaders communicate openly and transparently about challenges the organisation faces?* This behavioural focus ensures that the survey assesses not just the awareness of values but also the actions and behaviours that reflect those values.

The Value of a Tailored Approach

The ability to customise the 360 CPS is crucial, because no two organisations are alike. The values that work for one company might not be relevant for another. And even within the same industry, organisations have their own unique challenges, cultures, and goals. A tailored approach ensures that the culture measurement process is directly aligned with the specific cultural aspirations of the organisation's leadership.

Furthermore, this tailored approach can significantly improve the cultural alignment of different levels of the organisation. By identifying where cultural permeation is strong and where it is weak, leaders can take targeted action to reinforce the values and behaviours they want to see. Whether that involves additional training, clearer communication, or even restructuring teams, the 360 CPS provides the actionable insights necessary to foster a truly cohesive and aligned culture.

Beyond Measurement: Using the Results to Drive Change

Measuring culture is only the first step. The true value lies in how an organisation responds to the data it gathers. Once the 360 CPS identifies where cultural misalignments exist, leaders must act swiftly and decisively to address them. This could involve working with teams that are struggling to live out the organisation's values, providing coaching or mentorship for leaders who may not be modelling the expected behaviours, or revisiting the values themselves to ensure they resonate at every level of the organisation.

It's also important to recognise that culture is dynamic; it evolves over time, and regular reassessment is essential. The 360 CPS is designed to be used periodically, allowing organisations to track their cultural progress and make adjustments as needed. Culture isn't something you set and forget; it requires continuous attention, adjustment, and reinforcement.

Conclusion

In today's competitive landscape, having a clear, permeating culture is a crucial differentiator. The tools available in the market offer valuable insights, but measuring culture at the aggregate level often fails to provide the granularity needed to drive meaningful change. The 360 Culture Permeation Survey fills this gap, offering a tailored, level-by-level approach that gives leaders the information they need to ensure that their chosen values and behaviours are not just words on paper but lived realities across the organisation. By using this methodology, leaders can confidently measure, master, and embed the culture that will drive long-term success.

Reflection: Questions for Leaders

- Do you know if the culture you aspire to create truly exists at every level of your organisation?
- How often are you assessing cultural permeation across different leadership levels?
- Are your current tools for measuring culture tailored to your organisation's unique values and behaviours?
- When you identify cultural blockages, how quickly and effectively do you act to address them?

Chapter 10

Long Term Culture – Sustainable Practices for the Future

Culture, like any other aspect of an organisation, is not a 'set it and forget it' phenomenon. It requires ongoing attention, adjustment, and a conscious effort to ensure that it remains both relevant and sustainable over time. Without a long-term approach, even the most well-designed culture can erode or become misaligned with the evolving needs of the business. To embed culture as a long-term, sustainable aspect of an organisation, leaders must actively nurture it, ensuring that it's deeply integrated into every part of the business, from daily operations to long-term strategies.

The Importance of Longevity in Culture

Sustainable culture is one that can weather changes in leadership, economic shifts, and other external pressures. This means creating a culture that is resilient and flexible yet firmly rooted in values that remain consistent over time. Leaders must be forward-thinking and ensure that the culture not only meets today's needs but is adaptable enough to thrive in future environments.

A sustainable culture is often built on a foundation of continuous improvement. By creating mechanisms that allow for regular reflection, feedback, and adjustment, organisations can ensure their culture grows in line with their strategic objectives. This involves both fostering a learning mindset across the workforce and embedding an ethos of adaptability within the organisation.

Building Culture into Organisational DNA

For culture to be sustainable, it must be embedded in the organisation's DNA. This goes beyond simply having a set of values written down or discussed during onboarding. It requires that the organisation's culture becomes a part of how things are done every day, across all functions and at every level.

One powerful way to achieve this is by integrating culture into all core processes, recruitment, training, performance management, and succession planning. For example, when hiring, the focus should not only be on skills and experience but also on cultural fit. Do the candidate's values align with those of the organisation? How will they contribute to the overall culture, and how will they thrive within it? This is particularly critical when hiring senior leaders.

Likewise, when it comes to promotions and performance reviews, employees should be evaluated not just on their results but on how they embody and contribute to the company's values. In this way, culture is reinforced through the entire employee lifecycle, making it an enduring aspect of the organisation.

The Role of Leadership in Sustaining Culture

One of the most critical factors in long-term culture sustainability is leadership continuity and consistency. Senior leaders need to be the ongoing custodians of the culture, ensuring that it is lived out not only through their behaviours but also through their strategic decisions. They set the tone for the rest of the organisation and must demonstrate that culture is non-negotiable, even when the business environment becomes challenging.

A key responsibility of leadership in maintaining a long-term culture is ensuring that culture is always part of strategic conversations. Leaders must ask themselves, 'How does this decision impact our culture? Will this strategy align with the values we hold?' Embedding these cultural considerations into long-term planning and decision-making is essential for sustainability.

Leadership transitions are often a point where culture can be at risk. If a new leader arrives without a strong commitment to the organisation's values or without a clear understanding of its cultural foundation, the organisation can quickly find itself in cultural disarray. Succession planning that prioritises cultural alignment can help mitigate this risk.

Innovation and Culture Adaptation

Another vital component of a long-term culture is the ability to adapt to change without losing the core values that define the organisation. As markets evolve, as new technologies emerge, and as customer demands shift, organisations must innovate and adapt while still maintaining the integrity of their culture.

The challenge is to stay relevant without losing the essence of what makes the organisation unique. Leaders must strike a balance between preserving core cultural values and allowing for the flexibility needed to adapt. This requires a keen understanding of which aspects of culture are immutable and which ones can evolve to meet new circumstances.

Celebrating Milestones and Continuous Reinforcement

Sustainability also involves celebrating cultural milestones and achievements along the way. Recognising when the organisation lives out its values in meaningful ways reinforces those behaviours and ensures the culture stays top-of-mind. This could be as simple as acknowledging a team that has demonstrated exceptional integrity in the face of adversity, or more formalised through annual culture awards.

Over time, continuous reinforcement of cultural practices, paired with tangible recognition of those who uphold them, solidifies the importance of culture in the long term. As a result, employees feel more invested and aligned, and they're more likely to maintain and protect the culture as the organisation grows and evolves.

Sustaining Culture Through Governance and Policies

Governance plays a key role in sustaining a culture over the long term. A well-established set of policies, procedures, and governance frameworks that reflect the organisation's values helps institutionalise the culture. This ensures that even as people come and go, the core elements of the culture are preserved. These policies could cover areas such as performance evaluations, decision-making processes, communication protocols, and ethical standards, all of which should reinforce the desired culture.

The governance framework should not be seen as rigid or static. It must be flexible enough to adapt to changes in the organisation's environment while remaining grounded in the core values. As the organisation evolves, so too must its approach to governance, but the guiding principles should remain consistent. Leaders should regularly review these frameworks to ensure they continue to reflect the company's desired culture and are effectively supporting it.

Embedding Culture in External Relationships

Culture sustainability isn't just about what happens within the organisation. It extends to how the organisation interacts with external stakeholders, including customers, partners, and the community. Sustainable culture should be visible in the organisation's external relationships, as these interactions offer an opportunity to demonstrate cultural values in action. For example, a company that values transparency will communicate openly with customers and partners, sharing relevant information and being honest about challenges or setbacks.

Long-term culture is also reinforced by maintaining consistency in these relationships. If stakeholders perceive a gap between what the company claims its values are and how it actually behaves, trust is eroded. A strong culture will be reflected in ethical sourcing, fair partnerships, and corporate social responsibility (CSR) initiatives, where the organisation's values are lived out in the wider community.

The Role of Technology in Sustaining Culture

In today's digital world, technology can be an ally in maintaining a long-term organisational culture. Remote work, digital collaboration tools, and global teams are becoming the norm, and organisations must find ways to keep culture alive in a more dispersed workforce. Technology can be used to promote cultural alignment, whether through company-wide platforms for recognition and communication or through virtual town halls where leaders can connect with employees and reiterate the core values.

However, the challenge with technology is ensuring that it doesn't dilute the human element of culture. Leaders must find a balance between using digital tools to reinforce the culture and ensuring that personal interactions and authentic connections aren't lost. Tools like employee feedback platforms and performance management systems can be tailored to measure how well employees align with the organisation's values and provide real-time insights into how culture is perceived across various levels of the business.

Building Culture for a Multigenerational Workforce

Another important consideration for sustaining culture in the long term is addressing the needs of a multigenerational workforce. Today's workforce spans multiple generations, from Baby Boomers to Generation Z, each bringing different values, expectations, and working styles. A sustainable culture must be inclusive enough to engage all generations while still holding true to its core principles.

Leaders must be aware of these generational differences and seek ways to bridge gaps without compromising the organisation's fundamental culture. For example, younger generations might value flexibility, innovation, and social responsibility, while older generations might prioritise stability, loyalty, and clear processes. The challenge is creating a culture that accommodates these differences while ensuring that everyone is aligned with the overarching values and goals of the organisation.

Culture as a Competitive Advantage

In an increasingly competitive business landscape, a strong and sustainable culture can be a key differentiator. Companies with clearly defined, well embedded cultures often outperform those that lack this internal coherence. This is because culture shapes the employee experience, customer satisfaction, and even innovation.

A sustainable culture is one that consistently drives the organisation's performance. Employees are more likely to be engaged, motivated, and loyal when they see the organisation's values being upheld over time. Similarly, customers and partners are more likely to trust and remain loyal to an organisation whose values align with their own and that consistently demonstrates integrity and ethical behaviour.

Organisations with strong cultures can also be more resilient in the face of external challenges. Whether it's navigating economic downturns, regulatory changes, or industry disruption, a cohesive and well-maintained culture provides a solid foundation on which the business can rely. In this way, culture becomes not just a reflection of the organisation's internal environment but a strategic asset that drives long-term success.

Culture and Corporate Social Responsibility

Sustainability in culture also ties into corporate social responsibility (CSR) initiatives. An organisation that places a premium on its culture is likely to extend this focus to its impact on society. CSR practices, such as environmental stewardship, ethical business practices, and community engagement, often stem from an organisation's core values. By embedding these values into the company's operations and decision-making, organisations can ensure that they contribute to broader societal goals while also reinforcing their internal culture.

Leaders who are serious about sustaining culture should consider how their organisation's external initiatives, like sustainability programmes, philanthropy, and ethical governance, align with their cultural values. Not only do these efforts enhance the company's reputation, but they also create a more meaningful and purpose-driven environment for employees. When employees feel their organisation is making a positive impact on the world, they are more likely to be engaged and aligned with the culture.

The Role of Feedback in Culture Sustainability

One of the most effective ways to ensure the long-term sustainability of culture is by establishing continuous feedback loops. Employees should have regular opportunities to provide feedback on how well the culture is being upheld and how they experience the organisation's values in action. This can be done through surveys, focus groups, or one-on-one conversations with leadership. Gathering and acting on this feedback is crucial to maintaining a dynamic, healthy culture.

Leaders should not only collect feedback but also create a mechanism for responding to it. If employees feel their feedback is ignored, they may become disengaged or cynical about the organisation's cultural commitments. On the other hand, when feedback is valued and acted upon, it reinforces the culture by showing that the organisation is genuinely committed to living its values. This active listening approach allows the culture to evolve naturally and stay relevant to the workforce's needs over time.

Creating a Culture of Accountability

A sustainable culture is one where accountability is woven into the fabric of daily operations. Leaders and employees alike must be held accountable for living up to the organisation's core values and behaviours. However, accountability should not be punitive. Instead, it should focus on improvement and growth. Creating a culture of accountability ensures that the values aren't just aspirational but are actively shaping the decisions, actions, and performance of everyone in the organisation.

Accountability starts with the leadership team. Leaders must model the behaviours they expect from others and hold themselves to the highest standards. They should be transparent about their own challenges and missteps, using them as learning opportunities. When accountability becomes a shared responsibility, it fosters trust and commitment among employees, who feel that everyone – regardless of rank – is held to the same standard.

In practice, accountability can be embedded in processes such as performance reviews, team meetings, and project debriefs. Employees should have clear expectations of what is required of them, and there should be a mechanism for assessing whether those expectations are being met. By consistently reinforcing the importance of accountability, organisations ensure that their culture remains robust and aligned with their long-term vision.

The Importance of Role Models and Mentorship

For a culture to be sustained, organisations must cultivate strong role models who embody the values and behaviours of the desired culture. These individuals serve as living examples of what the culture looks like in action. They can be found at every level of the organisation, from top executives to middle managers to frontline employees. Having visible role models reinforces the idea that culture is not just a top-down initiative, but something that everyone can and should contribute to.

Mentorship plays a significant role in embedding and sustaining culture over the long term. Experienced leaders and employees can mentor newer team members, guiding them on how to navigate the culture and integrate the organisation's values into their work. These relationships create continuity, as knowledge and expectations are passed down from one generation of employees to the next. Mentorship also builds stronger connections within the organisation, enhancing engagement and loyalty.

Over time, organisations should also identify and celebrate their cultural ambassadors – people who naturally embody the culture and influence others positively. These ambassadors can lead by example, help onboard new employees, and keep the culture alive through everyday interactions.

Continuous Learning and Development for Cultural Sustainability

Long-term cultural sustainability depends on ongoing learning and development. As the world changes, organisations must adapt and their cultures must evolve with them. To prevent stagnation, organisations should create opportunities for continuous learning that reinforce the core values while allowing for innovation and growth.

This involves not only formal training programmes but also encouraging a mindset of lifelong learning. Employees should be given opportunities to develop new skills, take on new challenges, and experiment with new ways of working, all within the context of the organisation's values. Leaders, too, should be committed to their own development, seeking feedback from their teams, participating in leadership training, and staying informed about industry trends that could affect the culture.

By investing in learning and development, organisations not only help employees grow but also signal that they are committed to the long-term success of both individuals and the organisation. This sense of shared growth strengthens the cultural bond between employees and the company, making it more likely that the culture will endure over time.

Conclusion

A sustainable culture doesn't just happen. It is the result of deliberate effort and careful attention to the values, behaviours, and processes that make up the organisation's identity. By embedding culture into the core functions of the organisation, ensuring leadership is aligned and invested, and creating mechanisms for continuous adaptation and reinforcement, companies can build cultures that stand the test of time. In doing so, they not only foster a thriving internal environment but also position themselves for enduring success in an ever-changing world.

Reflection: Questions for Leaders

To ensure your culture remains sustainable for the long term, ask yourself:

- How is culture embedded in the core processes of our organisation?
- Are we continuously reinforcing and celebrating our values?

- How do we maintain cultural alignment during leadership transitions or significant changes?
- Do our leaders view culture as a strategic priority, and how are they modelling it consistently?
- Are we prepared to adapt our culture to future market demands while preserving our core values?

Conclusion

The Culture You Create is the Future You Build

The power of organisational culture can be viewed as the bedrock for long-term success. Culture is never neutral; it either supports or undermines performance. It's a powerful force that can actively drive an organisation toward success or, if misaligned, become a barrier to achieving its goals. Nor is it something that can be established through a single initiative or project. It is a dynamic force, shaped by the values, behaviours, and decisions of everyone in the organisation, starting from its most senior leaders.

The journey to building a thriving culture, as explored throughout this book, is one that requires intentional effort and sustained commitment. It's not enough to simply define a set of values. Leaders must live these values through their day-to-day behaviours, embedding them at every level of the organisation. Alignment between leaders is crucial, as any gaps or inconsistencies will quickly become evident and erode trust within the organisation.

When we discuss culture, we're not just talking about a 'nice-to-have' set of principles that improve employee morale. Culture, when properly nurtured, can be a strategic differentiator that drives innovation, performance, and growth. It determines how effectively your teams communicate, collaborate, and solve problems. More importantly, a strong and positive culture has a direct impact on employee engagement, retention, and overall organisational success. Studies show that companies with strong cultures consistently outperform their peers in terms of profitability, employee satisfaction, and long-term sustainability.

As organisations face increasing complexity and rapid changes in the global marketplace, it is vital that they cultivate a culture of adaptability. This ability to embrace change, to learn, and to grow in the face of challenges, ensures that the organisation remains resilient and innovative. In today's competitive environment, where disruption can happen overnight, a thriving culture becomes the foundation upon which sustainable success is built.

Furthermore, creating a culture where success is celebrated and where employees feel valued is equally critical. Recognition and appreciation reinforce positive behaviours, foster loyalty, and energise the workforce. These seemingly small actions help to embed a sense of belonging and pride in the organisation, further strengthening the culture. When employees feel that their contributions matter, they are more likely to go the extra mile and take ownership of the company's success.

On the other side of the coin, leaders must also be prepared to tackle difficult issues head-on. When culture demands change, it's essential to have the courage and clarity to act, whether it's addressing poor alignment, dealing with toxic behaviours, or making tough decisions about individuals who resist change.

The longer these issues are ignored, the more they undermine the cultural fabric of the organisation.

The challenge for leaders is not just to build a strong culture for today, but to ensure that it remains resilient and relevant for the future. This involves continually measuring and assessing the culture, not just at the aggregate level, but in terms of its permeation across every layer of the organisation. Through tools like the 360 Culture Permeation Survey, leaders can ensure that the values and behaviours that underpin the organisation are truly alive and consistent across teams, departments, and geographical regions.

In a world that is becoming increasingly complex, with employees spread across the globe and connected through digital tools, culture must evolve to meet new challenges. Leaders must ensure that the essence of the culture remains intact while embracing new ways of working, collaborating, and engaging with people.

Final Reflection

As we draw this journey to a close, it's important to recognise that organisational culture is not a static entity. It's a living, breathing force that must be nurtured, shaped, and guided at every level. The power of culture lies in its ability to transform not only how an organisation operates but also how it feels, both to those inside and those who engage with it from the outside.

Throughout this book, we've explored the critical role of leadership in shaping culture, the profound impact of clear and aligned values and behaviours, and the essential nature of open, honest communication. We've examined how adaptability, accountability, and trust can be leveraged to build a resilient and high-performing organisation. But perhaps most importantly, we've emphasised that culture is about people. It's about how we choose to interact, lead, and inspire one another.

Every senior leader reading this must understand that your organisation's culture is, ultimately, a reflection of you. It is your vision, your values, and your behaviour that will set the tone for everyone else. It's about how you decide to act in those pivotal moments, when faced with challenge or change, that your culture will either flourish or falter. You must be the chief cultural architect, the role model, and the driving force that continuously embeds and reinforces the values and resulting behaviours you've chosen.

But the power of culture doesn't stop with leadership. It ripples outward. From the moment you unite your leadership team around a shared set of values and behaviours, to the way you communicate those values across the organisation, to how you deal with the inevitable challenges that arise, every action counts. And when every level of your organisation is aligned with the culture you envision, the results are profound: engaged employees, thriving teams, strong business outcomes, and, ultimately, a sustained competitive advantage.

Think of culture not as a 'once and done' initiative but as an ongoing journey. It's a long-term investment, and like any investment, it requires patience, effort, and commitment. There will be moments when the culture needs to evolve, when old behaviours no longer serve the organisation's future. There will be times when you must course-correct or make difficult decisions to maintain the integrity of the culture you've built.

However, if you've taken one thing from this book, it should be this: culture is the single greatest lever you have to shape your organisation's destiny. It is the glue that binds strategy to execution, the engine that powers innovation, and the foundation upon which trust and success are built.

If you lead with intention, if you design a culture that encourages the best in your people, and if you remain adaptable and focused on the long term, your organisation will thrive, not just for the next quarter, but for years and decades to come.

So, as you close this book, remember: the culture you create is the future you build. Make it intentional. Make it inspiring. Make it last.

Bibliography

Amabile, T.M. and Kramer, S.J. (2011). *The Progress Principle: Using Small Wins to Ignite Joy, Engagement, and Creativity at Work*. Boston: Harvard Business Review Press.

Argyris, C. (1991). *Teaching Smart People How to Learn*. Harvard Business Review, May-June Issue.

BBC News (2021) *Post Office scandal: How did it happen?* Available at: https://www.bbc.co.uk/news/business-56718036 (Accessed: 14 October 2024).

Brown, B. (2018). *Dare to Lead: Brave Work, Tough Conversations, Whole Hearts*. New York: Random House.

Cameron, K.S. and Quinn, R.E. (2011). *Diagnosing and Changing Organisational Culture: Based on the Competing Values Framework*. 3rd ed. Upper Saddle River: Prentice Hall.

Cameron, K.S. (2012). *Positive Leadership: Strategies for Extraordinary Performance*. San Francisco: Berrett-Koehler.

Cameron, K.S. and Quinn, R.E. (2011). *Diagnosing and Changing Organisational Culture: Based on the Competing Values Framework*. San Francisco: Jossey-Bass.

Clampitt, P.G., DeKoch, R.J., and Cashman, T. (2000). *A Strategy for Communicating about Uncertainty*. Academy of Management Perspectives, 14(4), pp.41-57.

Covey, S.M.R. (2006). *The Speed of Trust: The One Thing that Changes Everything*. New York: Free Press.

Dahl, S. (2017). *Trust in the Workplace: The Key to Retaining Employees*. Harvard Business Review. Available at: HBR Trust Article [Accessed 16 Oct. 2024].

Deci, E.L. and Ryan, R.M. (2000). *The 'What'*.

Deloitte Insights (2020) *The Culture Framework*. Available at: https://www2.deloitte.com/us/en/insights/focus/human-capital-trends/2020/organizational-culture.html (Accessed: 14 October 2024).

Denison, D.R. (1996). *What is the Difference Between Organisational Culture and Organisational Climate? A Native's Point of View on a Decade of Paradigm Wars*. Academy of Management Review, 21(3), pp.619-654.

Denning, S. (2007). *The Secret Language of Leadership: How Leaders Inspire Action Through Narrative*. San Francisco: Jossey-Bass.

Dutton, J.E. and Spreitzer, G.M. (2014). *How to Be a Positive Leader: Small Actions, Big Impact*. San Francisco: Berrett-Koehler.

Edmondson, A.C. (2019). *The Fearless Organisation: Creating Psychological Safety in the Workplace for Learning, Innovation, and Growth*. Hoboken: Wiley.

Edmondson, A.C. (1999). *Psychological Safety and Learning Behaviour in Work Teams*. Administrative Science Quarterly, 44(2), pp.350-383. Available at: JSTOR [Accessed 16 Oct. 2024].

Forbes (2016) *Wells Fargo's Fake Account Scandal: A Timeline of Key Events*. Available at: https://www.

forbes.com/sites/antoinegara/2016/09/28/wells-fargos-fake-account-scandal-a-timeline-of-the-banks-key-events/?sh=4f4a24a24345 (Accessed: 14 October 2024).

Friedman, R.A. and Rosenman, R.H. (1974). *Type A Behavior and Your Heart.* American Journal of Public Health, 64(2), pp.138-140. Available at: AJPH (Accessed 16 Oct. 2024).

Gallup (2021) *State of the Global Workplace: Employee Engagement Insights.* Available at: https://www.gallup.com/workplace/349484/state-of-the-global-workplace-2021-report.aspx (Accessed: 14 October 2024).

Gallup (2017). *State of the Global Workplace.* Gallup.

Goleman, D. (1998). *Working with Emotional Intelligence.* New York: Bantam Books.

Hampden-Turner, C. (1994). *Corporate Culture: From Vicious to Virtuous Circles.* London: Hutchinson.

Harvard Business Review (2018) *The Leader's Guide to Corporate Culture.* Available at: https://hbr.org/2018/01/the-leaders-guide-to-corporate-culture (Accessed: 14 October 2024).

Heifetz, R., Grashow, A., and Linsky, M. (2009). *The Practice of Adaptive Leadership: Tools and Tactics for Changing Your Organisation and the World.* Boston: Harvard Business Press.

Heifetz, R.A. and Linsky, M. (2002). *Leadership on the Line: Staying Alive Through the Dangers of Leading.* Boston: Harvard Business Review Press.

Kahn, W.A. (1990). *Psychological Conditions of Personal Engagement and Disengagement at Work.*

Academy of Management Journal, 33(4), pp.692-724. Available at: Academy of Management [Accessed 16 Oct. 2024].

Kanter, R.M. (2009). *Supercorp: How Vanguard Companies Create Innovation, Profits, Growth, and Social Good*. New York: Crown Business.

Kegan, R. and Lahey, L.L. (2009). *Immunity to Change: How to Overcome It and Unlock the Potential in Yourself and Your Organisation*. Boston: Harvard Business Review Press.

Kotter, J.P. (1996). *Leading Change*. Boston: Harvard Business Review Press.

Kotter, J.P. (2012). *Leading Change*. Boston: Harvard Business Review Press.

Kouzes, J.M. and Posner, B.Z. (2012). *The Leadership Challenge: How to Make Extraordinary Things Happen in Organisations*. 5th ed. San Francisco: Jossey-Bass.

Lencioni, P. (2002). *The Five Dysfunctions of a Team: A Leadership Fable*. San Francisco: Jossey-Bass.

Mayer, R.C., Davis, J.H., and Schoorman, F.D. (1995). *An Integrative Model of Organisational Trust*. Academy of Management Review, 20(3), pp.709-734.

McKinsey & Company (2020) *The link between performance and organisational health*. Available at: https://www.mckinsey.com/business-functions/organisation/our-insights/the-link-between-performance-and-organisational-health (Accessed: 14 October 2024).

New York Times (2017) *Inside Uber's Aggressive, Unrestrained Workplace Culture*. Available at: https://

www.nytimes.com/2017/02/22/technology/uber-workplace-culture.html (Accessed: 14 October 2024).

O'Reilly, C.A., Chatman, J., and Caldwell, D.F. (1991). *People and Organisational Culture: A Profile Comparison Approach to Assessing Person-Organisation Fit.* Academy of Management Journal, 34(3), pp.487-516.

Patterson, K., Grenny, J., McMillan, R., and Switzler, A. (2011). *Crucial Conversations: Tools for Talking When Stakes Are High.* 2nd ed. New York: McGraw-Hill.

Robinson, S.L. (1996). *Trust and Breach of the Psychological Contract.* Administrative Science Quarterly, 41(4), pp.574-599.

Rogers, E.M. (2003). *Diffusion of Innovations.* 5th ed. New York: Free Press.

Schein, E.H. (2010). *Organisational Culture and Leadership.* 4th ed. San Francisco: Jossey-Bass.

Schein, E.H. (2013). *Humble Inquiry: The Gentle Art of Asking Instead of Telling.* San Francisco: Berrett-Koehler.

Schneider, B., Ehrhart, M.G., and Macey, W.H. (2013). *Organisational Climate and Culture.* Annual Review of Psychology, 64(1), pp.361-388.

Schneider, B., Gonzalez-Roma, V., Ostroff, C., and West, M.A. (2017). *Organisational Climate and Culture: Reflections on the History of the Constructs in the Journal of Applied Psychology.* Journal of Applied Psychology, 102(3), pp.468-482.

Schwartz, S.H. (2012). *An Overview of the Schwartz Theory of Basic Values.* Online Readings in Psychology and Culture, 2(1), pp.1-20.

Senge, P.M. (2006). *The Fifth Discipline: The Art and Practice of the Learning Organisation*. Revised ed. New York: Doubleday.

Stone, D., Patton, B., and Heen, S. (2010). *Difficult Conversations: How to Discuss What Matters Most*. New York: Penguin Books.

The Guardian (2021) *Post Office scandal timeline: from IT system faults to wrongful convictions*. Available at: https://www.theguardian.com/business/2021/apr/22/post-office-scandal-timeline-from-it-system-faults-to-wrongful-convictions (Accessed: 14 October 2024).

The Verge (2017) *Uber's company culture under scrutiny after harassment claims*. Available at: https://www.theverge.com/2017/2/21/14683776/uber-sexual-harassment-allegations-susan-fowler-blog (Accessed: 14 October 2024).

The Wall Street Journal (2019) *Wells Fargo: Anatomy of a Scandal*. Available at: https://www.wsj.com/articles/wells-fargo-anatomy-of-a-scandal-11558626558 (Accessed: 14 October 2024).

Weick, K.E. and Sutcliffe, K.M. (2015). *Managing the Unexpected: Resilient Performance in an Age of Uncertainty*. 3rd ed. San Francisco: Jossey-Bass.

www.ingramcontent.com/pod-product-compliance
Lightning Source LLC
Chambersburg PA
CBHW020203200326
41521CB00005BA/233